BABY PLAY

CONTENTS

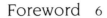

·FOREWORD·

Most of your baby's waking hours are spent at play. It is through playing that she comes to learn about herself and the world around her, and that she communicates and becomes attached to those who care for her. Her most enjoyable moments will be the ones she spends with you and I hope that this book will provide you with ideas and inspiration for making the most of your time together.

I have written this book for mothers, fathers, babysitters and all those who care for babies and are interested in finding out what current knowledge of development has to tell us about the sort of games and activities they enjoy. I use the phrase 'your baby' throughout to cover the various relationships which may be involved – from the strong commitment of parents to the less intense, but often sensitive and responsive, involvement of other caregivers. Your own baby may be a boy or girl and, accordingly, I have used 'he' or 'she' in alternate chapters.

In the Introduction, I describe how play forms the basis of the relationships a baby forms with those close to her, and how she brings her own special qualities to each encounter. Four sections follow, each covering a particular stage of the baby's life that has a clear identity of its own. First comes the period from birth to two months, when her instinct for learning and communicating becomes so apparent; then on to three months, a period characterized by disarming smiles and friendliness; next, four to seven months, a time of adventure and discovery; and lastly, eight to twelve months, when she may take her first steps and say her very first words.

Each section contains ideas for toys that fit in well with that particular stage of development. The main emphasis is on toys you can make yourself or adapt from everyday objects, but there are also descriptions of some of the more attractive ones you can buy, which are often well-designed from the point of view of child development and early learning. Finally, there are ideas for a wide range of activities that don't need anything more than just the two of you enjoying yourselves.

I hope you enjoy the book and find it useful. I would like to thank the staff at Frances Lincoln Ltd., especially Pippa Rubinstein, Gian Douglas Home and Caroline Hillier for their help and expertise in producing it; Edwina Riddell for her attractive illustrations and Nancy Durrell McKenna for her sensitive photographs.

Pat Petrie

The Nature of Baby Play

▪ ▪ ▪ ▪ ▪ ▪ ▪ ▪ ▪ ▪ ▪ ▪ ▪ ▪ ▪ ▪ ▪ ▪ ▪

Social play

Play is first and foremost social. It is something parents do instinctively with their babies from their very first days together. It's a wonderful way of getting to know each other and it paves the way for more meaningful communication at a later stage.

Even at the outset, though, parents and babies can communicate through play. In the past, research tended to concentrate on the relationship between mother and baby, seeing it as very much of a one way thing and recording such details as how often a mother spoke to her baby. Recently, their relationship has come to be seen as more of an interactive, reciprocal process, with mother and baby leading each other forward[1].

A baby is innately social – his smiles, his cries and the way his eyes catch and hold your own are all examples of his socially adaptive behavior. In all of his exchanges with you, you introduce him to different experiences, communicating your enjoyment and remaining open and attentive to what he has to convey to you. It may be you who start a game and keep it going with the little twists you know will hold his attention, or it may be that he attracts your attention to begin with and starts a whole sequence of play – smiling and babbling to you and before you know where you are, you're playing peek-a-boo around the side of his crib!

From his very earliest days, he will love to play – doing things just for the sake of doing them and the fun and pleasure it brings. However, play also has its purpose. Through it your baby learns about the properties of things around him, about himself and the people who play with him. He also has ample opportunity for experimenting with his developing abilities, and each new stage in his development opens the way for a variety of new games and activities. Physical games can become more robust once he can support his head and trunk; toys and household objects can be discovered and explored once he can reach out and grab hold of things successfully.

Play and the individual

The ideas given for games and activities in this book are chosen to correspond with your baby's developing physical and mental abilities, but are not guaranteed to suit every baby's emerging "personality". Even at this early age, your baby's own individuality will influence how he responds to the games you play together and soon he may start to show a preference for a particular type of game or activity.

Note: Superior figures in the text refer to References on page 124

Special characteristics

Although he follows the same regular pattern of development and has the same need for love and play as other babies, he is also truly unique. The reasons for his individuality lie in a variety of factors – inherited characteristics, pre-birth history, family circumstances, the relationships he forms with you and others, and the way these all interact with each other.

Each ovum and sperm carry a genetic message that is unmatched by any other ovum or sperm – even from the same mother or father. So, from the moment he is conceived, your baby is a unique individual (unless, of course, he happens to be an identical twin). The genes he inherits determine all sorts of things about him, most noticeable of which are physical characteristics such as hair and eye color and shape of features.

Nature or nurture?

Nobody yet knows, and perhaps we shall never know, to what extent any one child's intelligence is inherited from his parents and to what extent it is affected, for good or ill, by his experiences before and after birth. Each baby inherits a certain intellectual potential but how near he comes to fulfilling it will depend on the various experiences he meets on his way. The same can be said for temperament in the sense that both inherited characteristics and experiences encountered before and after birth play their part in forming his personality.

Studies involving sets of identical and non-identical twins suggest that some characteristics, such as being a specially active or rather passive child, are inherited because identical twins are alike in these ways and non-identical twins less so[2]. Caution, fearfulness and daring are other characteristics which also appear to be inherited. But, once again, inherited characteristics are only part of the story – how you and other people react to your baby and the sort of messages you give him about the way he interacts with the world around him are also important. You may experience an active, fearless baby as a potential explorer and watch proudly as he sets out to climb the stairs, or your anxiety for his safety may be uppermost. I remember my own mixed feelings of pride and worry when one of my sons showed that he could climb out of his crib or playpen before he was even a year old.

The extent to which your baby responds to different types of play will vary during the course of the day. The expression on his face will tell you much about his mood of the moment.

Babies do differ in so many ways. Yours may be constantly on the move, difficult to calm down and seeming to need less sleep than others; or cuddly, settling comfortably into your arms and responding quickly when you soothe him. He may take to new experiences easily, whether it's the taste of new food or meeting a new person, or actively resist certain new experiences, screwing up his face and turning away as a spoonful of food approaches. Or he may come between the two extremes – adopting a cautious approach and moving from hesitancy to reluctant acceptance of

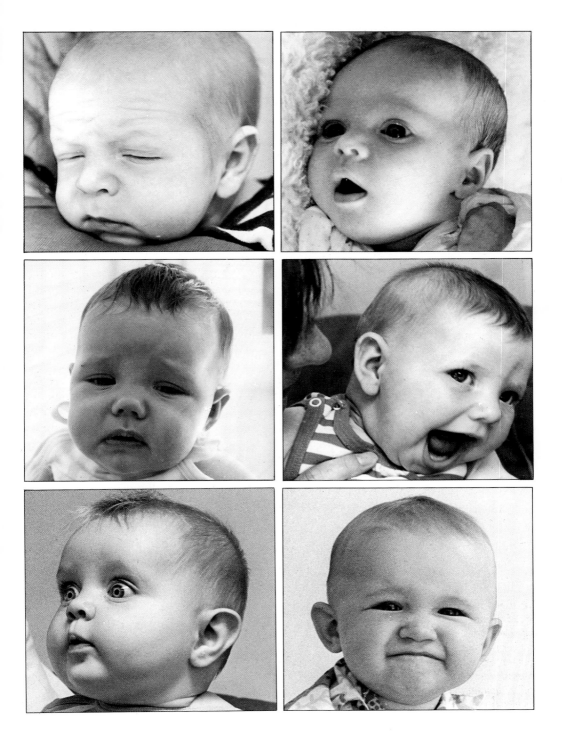

It's fascinating to watch a baby at play, using his developing skills in so many different ways and discovering which his particular talents are. From an early age, babies show their preference for a particular style of play. Some may prefer quieter games requiring concentration; others may prefer more energetic physical play.

new experiences. If you can accept him as he is, with the advantages and disadvantages that spring from his particular temperament, then he's off to a good start.

Different rates of development

In this book, I have aimed to give an outline of your baby's development from birth to twelve months, indicating the sequence of stages and approximate ages at which he can be expected to develop certain abilities and enjoy different forms of play. I'd like to emphasize, however, that development is in no way a simple, uniform process and that for a variety of reasons – whether genetic or as a result of experience, or a mixture of both – babies do not reach various milestones at the same age. For instance, there can be wide variation in the age at which a child will start to walk – he may do so at any time from eight or nine months to halfway through his second year – without there being any cause for concern. In the same way, a child can be very late in developing language and yet be intellectually normal, or even brighter than average. So although your baby will follow the basic pattern described in the following chapters, be prepared for him to do so at his own pace, reaching various points earlier or later than other babies you know of the same age.

Maturation – the regular sequence of changes which take place in the central nervous system from conception to maturity – is an important aspect of your baby's development, which, like growth and strength, develops rapidly in the first year of life. The central nervous system becomes more sophisticated and complex both in its structures and in the way it functions during the next twelve months, and the results can be seen in the progress your baby makes: his developing control over his movements, his first smiles and his growing understanding of life. Broadly speaking, the sequence of maturation is the same for all healthy children all over the world, and it is for this reason that psychologists have found it useful to view development in terms of basic stages, through which children pass in the same order[3]. In general, this can be said to be true of both physical and mental development.

Whether parents and other caregivers can speed up the course of maturation, is a question which psychologists have studied for many years. If, for example, a baby is given practice every day, is it possible to train him to sit up, or to walk, sooner than he would have done? The answer seems to be that it is possible to encourage him to do things rather earlier than he might have done if not encouraged, but that no advances can be made until he has reached the right level of maturity.

A famous experiment with identical twins encouraged one twin to practice stair climbing from an early age[4]. As a result, he did learn to climb the stairs earlier than his twin, but the latter very soon accomplished the same task without any extra practice! In both cases, maturation turned out to be more important than experience.

Although your baby can't be hurried on, he can be held back if he doesn't get enough opportunity to develop his potential. He won't learn to speak, for instance, unless someone talks to him, even though he – and his nervous system – are perfectly ready to do so. Fortunately, he has many ways of capturing your attention and engaging you in the sort of "conversations" and games that will give him the experience he needs.

Early influences on development

External factors can affect a baby's physical and mental condition at birth and how he develops in the first few weeks of life. If a mother is very undernourished during pregnancy, then her baby is likely to have a low birth weight, be less resistant to disease, and possibly less responsive than other babies at birth. The form the birth takes – whether it is by Caesarian section or with or without drugs – can also affect a baby's condition. In fact, mothers who are given certain drugs during delivery are more likely to give birth to babies who are sleepy and remain rather unresponsive during the first few weeks of life. This may also occur when babies are born prematurely.

Whether these early setbacks have a long-lasting effect on a child depends to a certain extent on how the baby is subsequently cared for. As a result of recent research, we now know that babies and young children have one reassuring characteristic – they are extremely resilient and, if well cared for, can recover from adverse experiences and make good progress[5]. I personally know of twins who were found starving and severely underweight in the South American jungle, but who were adopted at about a year old and are now bright, lively six year olds.

Cultural practices

Research into different cultural practices shows that society can and does affect the way in which babies develop. In the coastal districts of New Guinea, for example, babies learn to swim from a very young age so that once they are toddlers they can swim like fish[6]. Other more subtle influences on a child's development exist because of the ways in which society perceives and treats babies according to their sex. In our own society, studies have shown that parents often have different plans for a boy than for a girl, and that their perceptions of a baby may be different according to the baby's sex[7]. Fathers who had a brief glance at their babies through a glass screen just after birth, described the boys in such terms as "mischievous" while they spoke of the girls as being "pretty" or "cute". One researcher introduced babies, dressed carefully in unisex suits, to different adults and left them to decide the baby's gender[8]. The adults played in more lively and exciting ways with a "boy" and in more soothing ways with a "girl". Experiences such as these, repeated throughout his early years, can have a real effect on how a child comes to see himself and his place in the world, as well as influencing the type of games he comes to enjoy.

Caregivers

The part played by caring adults is vitally important for a baby's on-going development. After all, your baby presents you with all his potential for becoming a creative, loving human being and it is your sensitivity and responsiveness which help him to develop. In order to be happy, people need other people who know them, understand them and are responsive to their needs, and this is especially true of your baby. He needs your interest and involvement, just as much as he needs to be fed and changed and given a cosy crib and a warm room to sleep in. He needs to be attached to you.

As you get to know him, you will become increasingly sensitive to his changing moods and needs. From a very early age, you will notice how he passes from a state of quiet alertness, when he is particularly receptive and ready for play and talk, to one of energetic activity, with arms and legs waving wildly. Mothers, in particular, are sensitive to the quality of their baby's cries and what they mean. They are also quick to recognize signs that their baby is bored and in need of attention, or bewildered and overtired by a game that is too intense or that has gone on for too long. In contrast, a stranger who is not attuned to your baby's needs will not necessarily pick up his cues. I remember a young visitor who soon reduced a friend's baby to crying by shaking a rattle too vigorously and for too long in front of him.

However, people close to your baby can be very sensitive to him. Watch a father swinging his baby over his head and down to the ground and you will notice that the baby shows no signs of alarm. This is because the father is alert and sensitive to what his baby enjoys and what he finds threatening, as in all sorts of ways – tiny intakes of breath, gurgles of laughter, expectancy written on his face – the baby lets him know how high and fast he wants to go. For his part, the father communicates to his baby that he is in safe hands and great fun to be with.

Attachment

In the past, much emphasis was placed on mothers as the person to whom babies should be attached and, indeed, in the early months especially, mothers are very important. But psycho-logists now accept that other members of the family and friends can become attachment figures[9] – people to whom your baby can turn both for fun and for comfort in distress, and who can open his eyes to new things in the world around him and to different ways of relating to people. It is through interacting with a variety of different attachment figures in this way, that your baby develops

Gentleness and moments of closeness and intimacy are characteristic of the relationship between a father and his baby.

Grandparents often have a very warm, open relationship with their grandchildren. Their mutual responsiveness can be such that each feels totally relaxed and at ease in the presence of the other.

intellectually and learns many important social skills – how to get along with people, how to take turns in conversation and how to discover language and its uses.

Recent research no longer concentrates solely on mothers and babies to the exclusion of other close relationships. We now know more about the ways in which fathers relate to their babies with their own special styles of play and communication[10]. Other studies are beginning to look at relationships between babies and their brothers and sisters[11] and babies and other babies[12] and, although this research is still in its early stages, we are coming to

Changing views

Playful interaction
between a mother and
her young baby lays the
foundations for more
effective communication
in later months.

appreciate the importance that other children can have for a baby. If your baby has an elder brother or sister, life will be quite different for him – he will learn to share and will also have the benefit of a young companion.

Ideas about the place of babies in our society and the ways in which they should be cared for have undergone quite a transformation in recent years. Not so long ago, the advice for a young baby would have been that he should have a regular and fairly lonely routine of long spells between feedings, alone in his crib or carriage, away from other people and, except for the very worst weather, out of doors! It was not then understood that even the youngest babies can learn so much just from being with other people.

We are coming to realize more and more that a baby needs and enjoys company, and that leaving him on his own for much of the time, separate from other people, is to deprive him of many opportunities for play, talk and other experiences. This is not to say that he needs you to play with him constantly, just that he likes to be in the center of things; but he will also need times of peace and quiet, removed from too much noise and activity.

Taking care of yourself

Babysitters often care for two or three children at a time and can be remarkably skilled at finding the time to give each the individual attention that he or she requires.

There will also be occasions when you will want to have time for yourself, away from your baby. This is very understandable, and I hope that my enthusiasm for enjoying babies and being with them does not give you the impression that I think you should always be engrossed in your baby. All parents, and especially those who are trying to cope alone, need to get some rest and relaxation – time away from home perhaps, visiting friends, taking up threads of the life they were used to leading before the baby arrived. The first months after birth can be particularly tiring, and it is then more than at any other time that you may welcome the help and support

of those you know and trust – brothers, sisters and parents. At first, you may find it difficult to share your baby with others. You may worry that they will not be sensitive to his needs, his likes and his dislikes, but if you give them the chance to hold and get to know him, they will soon grow to understand him.

Working parents

Many mothers now return to work shortly after having their babies, and, as a result, the part played by caregivers from outside the family – babysitters and daycare attendants – has come under close scrutiny. The findings are encouraging for working parents, indicating that the baby will thrive as long as the caregiver is responsive and sensitive to his needs[13]. Even more encouraging is the knowledge that it is the quality of the time you as a parent spend with your baby that is crucial, rather than the quantity. It's your love and sensitive attention which forms the bond between you rather than the number of hours you spend in each other's company, although the time you spend together should be regular and frequent and something your baby can look forward to. If you do go out to work, the time you have to spend with your baby in the evenings and at weekends is very precious, and I have found, as a working mother, that it is worth letting my standard of housekeeping slide in order to have more time with my children.

Play and your daily routine

Even when you are able to be at home with your baby, there are bound to be competing demands on your time. You may, for example, want to have a conversation with another adult, get on with the cooking or see to the needs of an older child, or spend a few quiet moments by yourself. At times like these, you will only be able to give a small part of your attention to your baby, although you may find yourself keeping up a certain level of communication with him, through smiles, words and touch – stopping to talk as you pass by or reaching out a hand to stroke or tickle.

As you become more experienced, you will find countless small ways of continuing play throughout the routine tasks of daily life. After all, play is not simply about those times when you can give your undivided attention to a game, it's also about involving your baby and introducing him to seemingly mundane tasks in an enjoyable way. Letting him watch while you do the dishes hardly merits the status of a game, but it can be fascinating for your baby as he listens to the sounds of clattering cutlery and plates and watches intrigued as you lift each object, wet and glistening, from the water.

When you play together, try to see the world from your baby's point of view. For him, the present is all important; he doesn't plan for the future, nor think about the past. What he experiences in the present moment is everything to him, whether it's anger, boredom, enjoyment or just the comfort of being held close.

FIRST IMPRESSIONS

· · · · · · · · · · · · · · ·

0 – 2 MONTHS

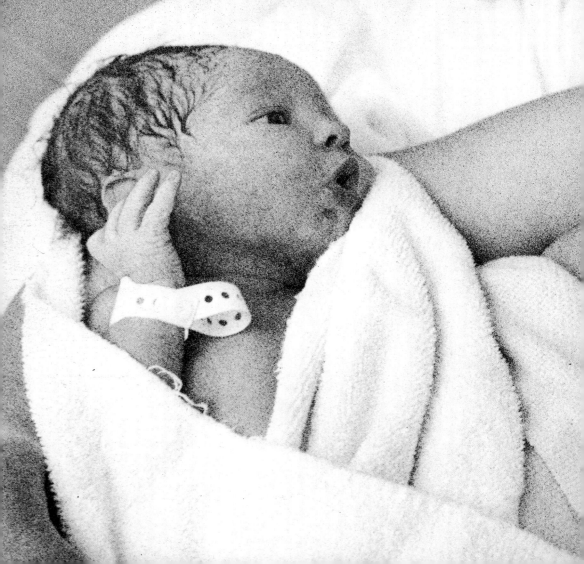

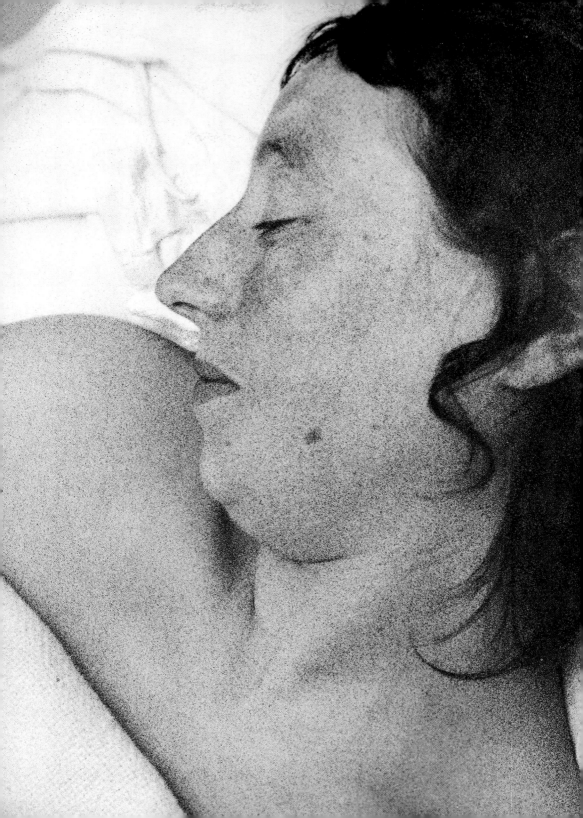

Introduction . . . .

Birth brings dramatic changes for your baby. In the world outside the womb, she experiences light and movement, clear sounds and the first sweet taste of milk. Suddenly she has ample space for kicking and arm waving, in complete contrast to the constant environment of your womb where she was surrounded by shock absorbing water and total darkness, and listened only to the regular, rhythmic sounds of your heartbeat, the gurgles of your digestive system and the occasional muffled sound of your voice and other sounds from the outside world. At birth, she is suddenly aware of many new, interesting sensations and the comforting, reassuring feeling of being held, touched and stroked.

A new relationship

How you feel during these first moments together will depend to some extent on what has gone before and how difficult or easy your labor has been. You may feel love for your baby from the moment you are first given her to hold in your arms, and embark straight away on a voyage of mutual discovery. But it may be that the experience of birth has left you tired and low and that at present you have little energy left for getting to know her. If she has a

Lifting her head for the first time gives her quite another perspective on life.

medical problem, you may only get a glimpse of her before she is taken away for special attention and nursing, and have to face the depressing prospect of not being able to be with her for quite some days, or even weeks. It's very disheartening if things turn out this way, but one way of coping is to concentrate all your energies on getting your strength back so you are better able to help your baby adapt to life when you are finally able to take her home.

If it is your first baby, you may feel nervous about handling her, unsure of what she needs and wants from you and, most disturbing of all, worried that you do not feel any immediate feelings of love or protectiveness towards her. If you experience these feelings, don't let them worry you: they are common reactions and unlikely to last once you start to get to know her and gain confidence in your ability to care for her.

The road ahead

She seems so helpless in so many ways – unable to support her head and with no understanding of speech and little experience of life – and yet she is astoundingly competent. She is equipped in many ways to learn about the world and will start to do so right from the moment of birth. You can help her just by being responsive and sensitive to her changing needs and by providing her with the opportunities she needs to learn.

Over the next few months, her vision will improve and she will soon be able to lift her head and absorb her surroundings and, perhaps most rewarding of all, she will delight you with her first smile. These first couple of months are a wonderful time for enjoying each other and for indulging in gentle games and 'conversations' together.

• ACQUIRING PHYSICAL SKILLS •

Most of the movements your newborn baby makes are reflexes: automatic responses to outside stimuli that are beyond her control. Towards the end of the first month, she shows signs of her developing muscular control when she lifts her head from the floor for the first time.

Reflexes . . . .

Some of your baby's reflexes will disappear during the first few months after birth as her central nervous system becomes more mature and higher levels of the brain come into use; others, such as blinking and coughing, will remain with her throughout life. Of those which disappear shortly after birth, some, such as the grasping and Moro reflexes (see page 28), seem of no immediate use to your baby but may well be left over from a much earlier stage of evolution when they would have given human babies a better chance of survival.

Your baby's development is not just a simple case of more advanced movements taking the place of simple movements and basic reflexes. In some cases, there may be quite a gap between when an early movement pattern or reflex disappears and a more advanced form of the same behavior takes over. This is so with her impressive attempts to grasp hold of things she can see – sometimes successful if her head is properly supported! – which disappear at about 4 weeks and do not reappear for another four months or so. The walking reflex also disappears early on and she

The baby's reflexes

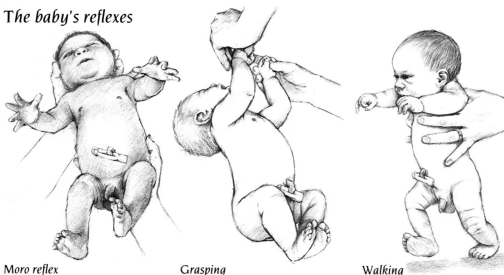

Moro reflex
Fear of being dropped makes a baby throw out his arms and open his fingers, closing them as he brings his arms back across his body.

Grasping
Stroke your baby's palm with your finger or thumb and he will grasp hold of it. For a short while after birth, he can support his weight by grasping.

Walking
If you hold a baby under his arms, with the soles of his feet touching a hard surface, he will automatically start to step forward.

Rooting and sucking
If you touch your baby's cheek with your nipple or a bottle, he will root for it, turning his head and opening his mouth (right). Taking the nipple well back into his mouth, he will begin to suck (far right).

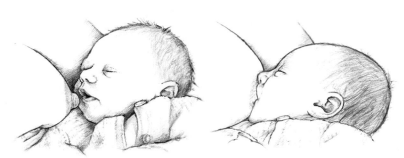

will not attempt to walk again until much later in the first year.

In other cases, movements which appear as controlled reactions to unpleasant experiences are in reality reflexes. For example, when a baby responds to a tissue being placed over her face by trying to remove it with her hand, this is in fact an anti-smothering reflex. Similarly, when she uses one foot to remove an irritating substance from her other leg, this is another defensive reflex.

Developing head control . . . .

She soon starts to develop muscular control, most noticeable during the first few months in her growing ability to support her own head. At first, if you turn her on her tummy, you will notice that her neck muscles are not yet strong enough to raise her head from the surface it is resting on. The necessary strength develops quickly and by the time she is a month old, she can lift her head momentarily at first, and then for increasing lengths of time. Throughout this period, she will need you to support her head when you pick her up and will welcome such support as you carry her around in this way, as it gives her the opportunity to observe her surroundings from a better viewpoint.

· PERCEIVING THE WORLD ·

We now know that a baby can react to noise, light and touch in the womb, so it's no longer so surprising that at birth these senses – hearing, sight and touch – are well-developed and actively at work. As well as these 'external' senses through which your baby comes to learn about the world around her, there are also her 'internal' senses which pick up information coming from within her body. One such sense tells her where the jointed parts of her body are in relation to one another when she moves; others alert her to cry for help when she feels hunger, discomfort or pain. All of these senses function in a similar way. The information they pick up is passed to the brain for interpretation and in this way your baby's knowledge of the world is formed.

For the moment, you are her richest source of sensory experience: as you hold her closely in your arms and let her suck vigorously to satisfy her hunger, as you clean and dry her and tuck her snugly in her crib and maybe stroke and sing to her. Through all these loving, caring acts, she comes to know you – your particular smell, your face and voice – and starts to feel secure in her new world.

When you play with her and involve all her senses, she experiences the enjoyment of doing things just for fun, just as she does when you whisper in her ear, talking and acting as if she understands every word you say, or imitate her funny faces – the way her tongue moves in and out and the tremble of her lower lip. She loves all these playful repetitions and will keep you going with her attentive gaze.

Seeing

At birth, your baby's eyesight is well-developed – she can see things in three dimensions and already has very acute visual discrimination and some notion of depth. But, as yet, she is only able to focus on objects about 20 cm (8 in) away from her, anything nearer or farther away is blurred. This limited focusing ability appears geared to her survival as a social being, as the distance at which she focuses best is about the distance between her eyes and the face of whoever is feeding her. In this way she comes to know and respond to the faces of those who care for her.

What babies like to look at

The human face, more than any other object, holds a very special attraction for a newborn baby. This is not surprising since it contains all the visual elements that a baby of this age finds most attractive – sharply defined outlines, changing expressions and the striking contrast of bright, shiny eyes which are constantly moving and catching the light. She's best able to focus on you when she's calm and alert after a feeding and at times like these she will gaze at your face with rapt attention. Give her time to absorb as much as she wants to, gently smiling or talking to her occasionally, but essentially making this a quiet time for you both. A baby of this age already shows a distinct preference for her mother's face but will quickly come to recognize other familiar faces too, indicating that her memory is already active[14].

Movement, change and contrast in her surroundings will capture her attention too, and in a darkened room her eyes will dart around searching for areas of light. She actively searches for things to look at and, finding something of interest, is capable of concentrating on it for quite some time. The sight of curtains hanging in shadow in contrast to the brightness of a nearby window will fascinate her, especially if the curtains are moving gently in the breeze.

Developmental psychologists have suggested that a young baby's interest in edges and outlines comes from her need to place objects visually in their environment before investigating further[15]. Even at this early age she is able to appreciate patterns of a fairly simple nature, but it is their contours and outlines which hold her attention rather than the inner details. One experiment showed clearly that during the first month babies prefer gazing at a two by two checkerboard but by two months they already prefer the more complex pattern of an eight by eight checkerboard[16]. At this age, it

Although this month-old baby is too young to understand that the toy placed in front of her is a cuddly bear, her attention is captured by the striking contrast of black and white.

is not the pattern as a whole which interests them, only the boundaries it contains and the striking contrast between the different colored squares.

Tracking a moving object

Your baby is fascinated by movement and is already capable of following a slowly moving object with her eyes. If you hold a brightly colored rattle in front of her, shake it to attract her attention and then, once she has had time to focus, move it slowly from one side of her head to the other, keeping it within her visual range, you'll be able to see her following it with her eyes. Not only is she keeping track of the rattle but she's also taking in information about its size, shape and color – a lot of information for her to deal with, so don't be surprised if she lets you know she's had enough of this game after a short while only.

Hearing . . . .

A baby's hearing is almost as acute as an adult's at birth, and when only a few minutes old she will look towards a sound expecting to find the source. Once you feel she is sufficiently relaxed and settled in her new environment, you can try lying down beside her with your head close to her ear and speaking to her in a gentle voice, making sure you are out of her visual range. You'll notice that her eyes will dart around to find the source of the voice and, in time, she may actually turn towards you. Your baby may become distressed if she can hear your voice but is unable to see you, so reassure her by letting her see your face.

What babies like to listen to

Just as they prefer the human face, babies seem to be more responsive to the human voice than to any other sound. They are particularly attracted by its pitch and are fascinated by its wide repertoire of sounds and the way it changes speed. Research has shown that a baby can actually distinguish between such similar sounds as 'pa' and 'ba'[17]. In fact, whichever language group a baby is born into, she can distinguish the different sounds which make up its words. Some research actually suggests that a baby will respond to an adult's voice with tiny movements, each corresponding to the different sounds contained in the words[18].

Initially a baby shows a distinct preference for her mother's voice. This may be due to the fact that her hearing is already well developed in the womb so she has had time to become familiar with the muffled sound of her mother's voice before birth. In one fascinating study, pregnant mothers who read aloud a particular story twice daily during their last six weeks of pregnancy had babies who showed a preference for that story over others when it was read to them a few days after birth[19].

Babies seem to enjoy music, particularly if it has a regular rhythmic beat and is not too loud, and will show their appreciation by becoming calm and attentive. At times your baby may prefer gentle, muted sounds such as those produced by a wooden rattle or chime bar, but her preference for loud or soft music will depend not only on her mood and temperament but also on what she is used to listening to. All of my own babies were perfectly at home with the sound of a full symphony orchestra on stereo from only a few days after birth, possibly because they had become accustomed to such sounds while in the womb.

Singing to your baby while you gently rock her is an experience she is bound to enjoy. Making songs and lullabies a regular part of your evening routine will help to pattern your baby's day.

For toweling after a bath, you can try:

Rub-a-dub dub,
Three men in a tub,
And who do you think they be?
The butcher, the baker, the candlestick maker,
And out they go, all three.

For settling to sleep, a quiet lullaby:

Twinkle twinkle little star,
How I wonder what you are,
Up above the world so high,
Like a diamond in the sky.

Toys to see and hear
Your baby appreciates any opportunity to use her developing sight and hearing, but at this age she is often placed in her crib lying on her front with her head to one side, or settled on her back where she can only hold her head in a midline position for a few seconds before it falls to one side or the other. This is fine for sleeping, but when awake her view is very limited. You can make this time more interesting for her by placing a brightly colored toy or picture within her visual range, either hanging over the edge of the crib or tied to the side or simply tucked in against the side of the mattress.

As your baby's sight improves, you can increase the distance at which you position the objects, and once she is able to keep her head in a midline position (by about the second month), start to hang toys over her crib. You can buy rods of adjustable width that will fit across a crib or clamp to the sides and from which you can hang various colorful, interestingly shaped household objects or toys (see page 33). Mobiles — homemade or otherwise — can be hung from stands which are specially designed to clamp to the side of a crib or stroller. The advantage of buying such equipment is that it enables you to change the selection of crib and stroller toys before your baby has a chance to get bored with them.

Mobiles

Your baby's love of movement and contrast makes brightly colored mobiles the perfect toy for these first couple of months. There are some very attractive ones for sale, but you can easily make your own by hanging a variety of different colored objects of different shapes and sizes from a coat-hanger. There's no point in going to great lengths to make some intricately complex mobile as your baby is unlikely to appreciate it. As long as it contains contrast and color and objects of varying shapes and sizes, your baby will find it enchanting. Brightly colored strips of cloth or handkerchiefs and simple cut-out paper shapes attached to a single thread make a very attractive mobile.

Mobiles hung in different places will keep her captivated with their colors and sounds.

Your baby cannot yet use her hands to pull things down and put them in her mouth, so it is safe to display a range of household

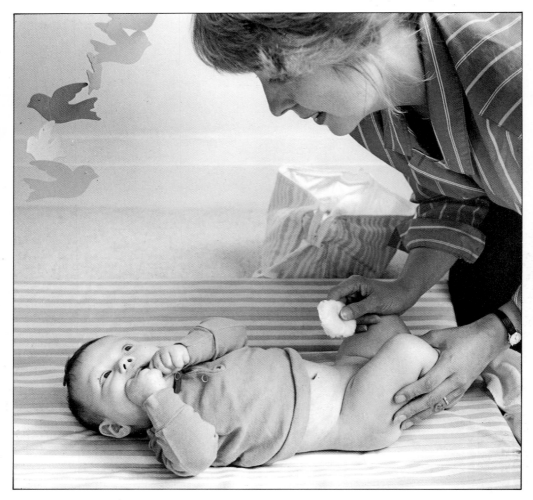

Hanging and changing toys

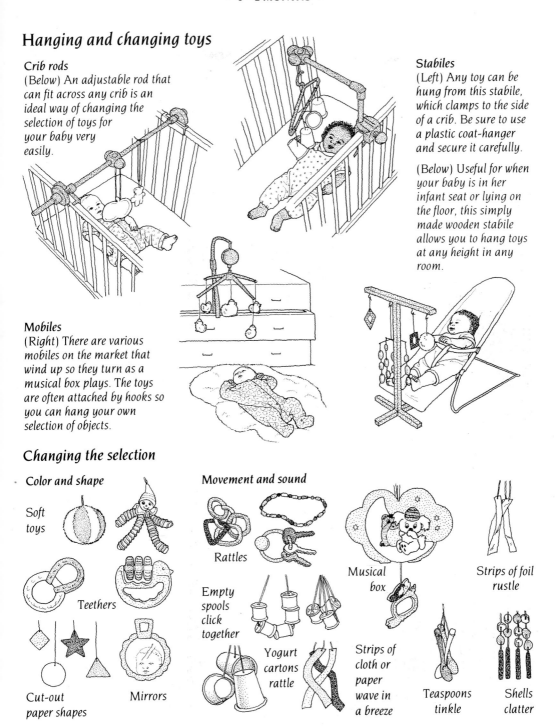

Crib rods
(Below) An adjustable rod that can fit across any crib is an ideal way of changing the selection of toys for your baby very easily.

Stabiles
(Left) Any toy can be hung from this stabile, which clamps to the side of a crib. Be sure to use a plastic coat-hanger and secure it carefully.

(Below) Useful for when your baby is in her infant seat or lying on the floor, this simply made wooden stabile allows you to hang toys at any height in any room.

Mobiles
(Right) There are various mobiles on the market that wind up so they turn as a musical box plays. The toys are often attached by hooks so you can hang your own selection of objects.

Changing the selection

Color and shape

Soft toys

Teethers

Cut-out paper shapes

Mirrors

Movement and sound

Rattles

Empty spools click together

Yogurt cartons rattle

Musical box

Strips of cloth or paper wave in a breeze

Strips of foil rustle

Teaspoons tinkle

Shells clatter

objects on a home-made mobile, as long as it is secured safely and well out of her reach. This type of mobile is no longer suitable once your baby is able to reach out and grasp hold of objects.

Don't forget that your baby will search for the source of a sound with her eyes so a mobile will have more to offer her if it is made out of materials which make a distinctive sound when they come into contact with one another.

Making things happen

Some of the more entertaining toys for your baby are ones that she can activate herself. There are various toys on the market which can be attached to the side of the crib by suction and which will rock and make a noise when your baby moves or kicks. Others can be strung across the crib and will rattle if your baby hits or kicks them – this will be accidental at first but she will soon enjoy making it happen. These types of toy help her to realize that through her actions she can have an effect on her environment.

Household objects are just as fascinating for your baby as specially bought toys.

Tuning out

Your baby may, at first, be very attentive to something new and interesting but may then quickly become used to it and lose interest. She may be absorbed by the sight and sound of someone clicking their fingers for instance, but after only a short while will refuse to pay any further attention. Your baby 'tunes out' in this way because she has learned all she can from this experience and is ready to move on to something new, not because she is tired and no longer able to pay attention.

When playing with her, it's important to be sensitive to the cues she gives you so that you come to recognize this 'tuning out' as the ideal moment for introducing a slight variation to the game you are playing, or for adding one or more new elements to an otherwise familiar mobile. But take care not to overwhelm her with too many changes too rapidly and always give her time to get used to and enjoy something she finds interesting before introducing any variation.

A change of scene

Toys and pictures wedged into the side of her crib may hold her attention for a short while but she'll soon let you know she's bored by crying for your attention. If you're too busy to stop and play with her, try bringing her stroller or infant seat into the kitchen or wherever you are working. This will give her a comfortable feeling of being in the center of things and you can chat to her as you work.

Prop her up in the corner of an armchair or settee supported by cushions or, even better, settle her securely on a bean bag, so she has a good view of everything going on around her and can watch you as you work. It'll be another couple of months yet before she starts to wriggle so you needn't worry about leaving her in one of these positions. It's well worth investing in one of the increasing range of specially designed, reclining infant seats available. You can place it on the kitchen table when you're cutting up the vegetables or beside you when you're doing the dishes. The common lightweight bouncing chair is not suitable for placing on worktops or tables and should only be placed on the floor. Your baby will usually be quite happy to sit back and watch you; after all, everything is new to her at this stage and she will be fascinated by your movements. *Do not, however, leave her unsupervised.*

When choosing an infant seat, consider the following points:
- if you want to place it alongside you on a worktop, make sure that the base of the seat is firm and secure enough to do so; rubber stops will prevent skidding
- if you want to be able to take it with you when you move from room to room, make sure that it is light enough for you to carry
- if you intend to use it for a very young baby, check that it is well-padded and slants far enough back to provide the maximum amount of security and comfort

Choosing an infant seat

Decide on the following before you make your choice:
Is the seat stable and safe? Does it clean easily? Is it light enough to be carried around easily? Do you want it to rock? Do you want it to be adjustable so that it lasts?

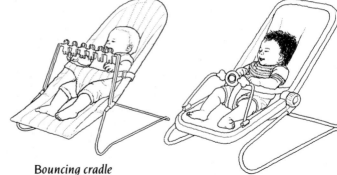

Bouncing cradle
(Above) The harness on this bouncing cradle is comfortably padded. She'll enjoy being bounced and soon she'll bounce herself.

Bouncing recliner
(Above) This can be used as a bouncing cradle to begin with and later adjusted so that your baby can sit in an upright position.

Easy chair/car seat
(Above) Highly adaptable, comfortable and easy to carry around, this seat is ideal for a young baby. It can be secured in a car, and then, while the baby sleeps, simply transferred to the house without waking her.

Reclining infant seat
(Left) This low seat can be adjusted to any of four positions, from the first, which is suitable for a young baby to lie in, to upright. The seat's feet fold under, making it into a rocking chair.

Household sights and sounds

Settling her in one of the above positions will give her a good opportunity to start exploring her surroundings. Remember to position her so that areas of vivid contrast and movement are within her visual range. Sunlight filtering through a window or a toddler playing with brightly colored toys are the sort of sights which will immediately capture her attention, combining contrasts of brightness, color and movement.

There will normally be plenty for your baby to listen to. Ordinary household sounds – a whistling kettle, the clink of a spoon or the wail of a vacuum cleaner – all catch her attention, and you will notice her becoming alert and paying attention when she hears them. But only the sound of human voices will keep their fascination for her. Remember that there will be times when she has had too much noise and bustle and will show you this by starting to fuss or cry, welcoming a quiet cuddle or the comfort and security of her crib.

A busy kitchen can provide endless entertainment for a young baby with its wide variety of sights and sounds, but make sure she's placed well out of harm's way!

Taste and smell . . . .

A baby's sense of taste and smell are closely connected and both appear to be well-developed at birth. In fact her likes and dislikes at birth appear so similar to an adult's that they are thought to be innate. A newborn baby will turn her head away from an unpleasant smell, and research has shown that at only a week old she can differentiate the smell of her mother from that of another woman[20]. She also shows a preference for sweet things and may smile when given something sweet to taste; in contrast, she will purse her lips at a sour taste and draw down her mouth at the corners at a bitter taste.

An interesting experiment has shown how babies aged only a day old show a distinct preference for sweet things[21]. The experiment was set up so that when a bell sounded the babies were rewarded with a few drops of sugary water if they turned their heads to the right, but were given no reward if they turned their heads when a buzzer sounded. They soon learned to ignore the buzzer and only respond to the bell, showing not only an innate preference for sweet things, but also an early ability to discriminate between one sound and another and to co-ordinate hearing, taste and movement into one meaningful action. Most interesting of all is the indication this experiment gives that they are already able to act on what they have learned from experience.

Your baby will be aware of different smells as you carry her from room to room. Smells of soap, talcum powder and toothpaste in the bathroom; peeled orange, a chicken roasting or bread baking in the kitchen. When you take her out into the garden or to a nearby park, she will experience other potent smells – whether of flowers or mown grass.

Touch . . . .

A newborn baby's skin is covered in touch receptors in varying densities, concentrated in areas like the mouth and hands and more widely spread in areas like the back. Her skin is the largest sensory organ in her body and through it she is able to enjoy the warmth, closeness and comfort that comes with physical contact.

Outside on a warm day, your baby will love to lie naked – kicking and playing – with you close beside her. Sensitive to touch on every level, she will love to hold your finger and kick against your body.

At this early age she will be very sensitive to changes in temperature and will need to be introduced gently to the idea of being without clothes. On a warm day when she's used to the idea, you can let her lie for a short while with no clothes on – not even a diaper – so she can enjoy the feeling of warm air on her skin and make use of the freedom of space to practice kicking. Even if the weather is cold, you can let her have a good kick with no diaper on in a warm room.

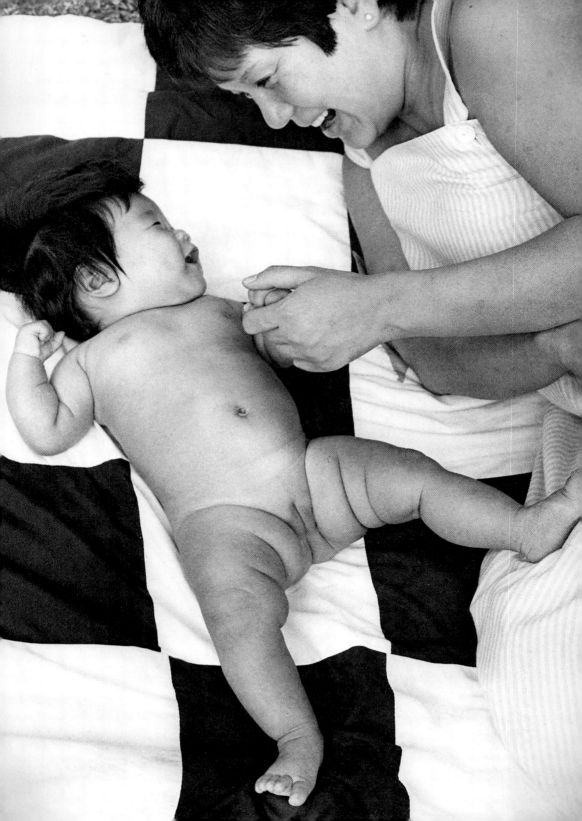

At present, she relies on you to provide her with opportunities for developing her sense of touch. You can take advantage of her grasping reflex while it lasts and place objects of different textures and shapes within her grasp. Give her the chance to get to know the feel of ordinary household things – alternate the warm, soft feel of a piece of cloth with the hard, cold texture of a teaspoon.

The value of physical contact

Physical contact is important for your baby's sense of well-being and she will love lying next to your skin with just a diaper on, perhaps when you are having a leisurely rest in bed. Some interesting research carried out on animal behavior suggests that babies may actually need an adult more for the physical contact and security they can provide than for their ability to feed them[22].

In the developed world, we have grown increasingly aware of the benefits of massage for health and well-being and how babies can benefit too, but in other cultures this has long been taken for granted. For many Afro-Caribbean and Indian parents, oiling and massage are a regular part of childcare. Baby massage is, of course, only an enjoyable extension of the touching that occurs naturally between parents and children.

Stroking and massage are very natural and direct ways of communicating tenderness for another person and so are ideal ways of helping your baby learn to feel relaxed and happy in the outside world. And, as well as emotional considerations, there are other advantages:

- premature babies who are touched and stroked make better progress than those who aren't – their heartbeat noticeably increases in response to the contact
- stroking and massage help relax muscles, producing a sense of well-being and calm
- stroking, touching and massage stimulate the baby's developing awareness and enjoyment of her own body
- massage is very beneficial to the circulation, skin, joints and digestive system and may help a baby who is suffering from colic

Oiling and stroking

It is best to wait until a baby is a month old before starting systematic massage. When she is younger, oiling and stroking while you talk softly and soothingly is enough. Choose a time no sooner than half an hour after feeding and make sure the room is warm and free of drafts. Settle comfortably on the floor or on a bed, either with your feet up supporting the baby on your thighs with her face towards you, or kneeling with her before you. Spread a towel underneath your baby before you begin. Have at a safe distance a bottle of baby oil warming in a pot of hot water and some tissues to mop up with if necessary.

Oil your hands, making sure that the oil is not too hot, and stroke your baby firmly but gently all over. Slowly rub the warm oil

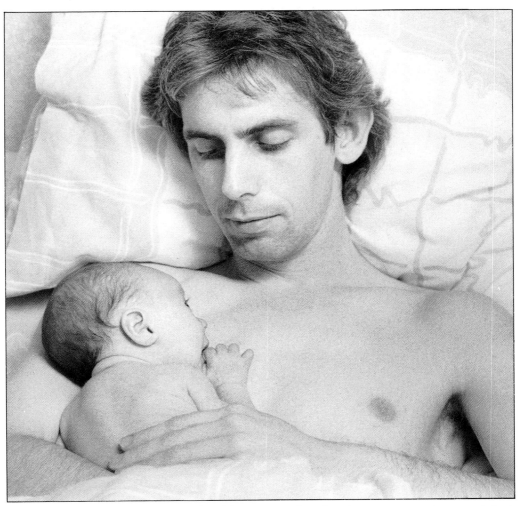

Touching and stroking are powerful ways of communicating. Here father and daughter are getting to know one another in a moment of quiet relaxation.

Massage

into her shoulders, arms, hands, chest, tummy, legs and feet. Always stroke away from the center of the body, *never* towards the heart, and until it's healed, avoid the navel. If she cries at first don't worry, just pick her up and comfort her. It takes some babies a while to enjoy being naked and she may feel a little insecure at first. Remember that this should be a pleasant time for both of you, so if she isn't enjoying it stop and try again another day.

When she is a month old you can introduce gentle massage of the chest, arms, abdomen, legs, back and face as shown in the illustrations on the following pages. By now your baby should be feeling more at home in the world and you may both want to make massage a regular feature of your time together.

Massaging your baby

Find a position that is comfortable for you both. You may like to kneel or sit cross-legged with your baby in front of you, or you may find it easier to sit with your legs stretched out in front of you and your baby lying lengthways along your thighs. Try to keep your movements slow and rhythmic, applying a gentle, even pressure.

Chest

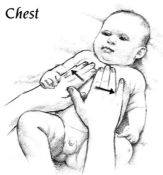

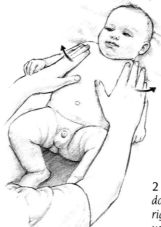

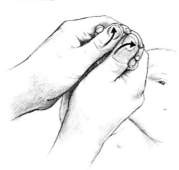

1 Oil your hands and put a few drops of oil on your baby's chest. Move your hands slowly outwards across his chest to either side of his body. Repeat the movement.

2 Bring your left hand slowly down from his left shoulder to his right side. Repeat this motion by moving your right hand down from his right shoulder to his left side.

Arms

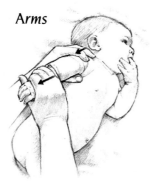

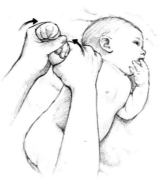

Hands

1 Place your baby on his side. Hold his shoulder with one hand and his wrist with the other. Bring your hand up his arm towards his wrist. Repeat the movement with your other hand.

2 Grasp his arm with both hands and work them, gently twisting each in the opposite direction to the other, up the length of his arm to his hand, before starting again from the shoulder.

Hold your baby's wrist with both hands and massage first his palm, working with your thumbs towards his fingers. Then massage his fingers as you unfold them.

Abdomen

1 Massage your baby's tummy downwards from the chest to the abdomen, one hand following on closely after the other, both moving in the same direction.

2 Then hold his feet up with one hand and continue the tummy massage further with your other hand, still following the same direction.

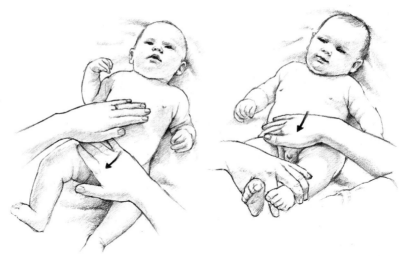

Legs

1 As with the arm massage, grasp the leg and bring your hands, one after the other, up his leg to his foot.

2 Twist your hands gently in opposite directions up the length of his leg.

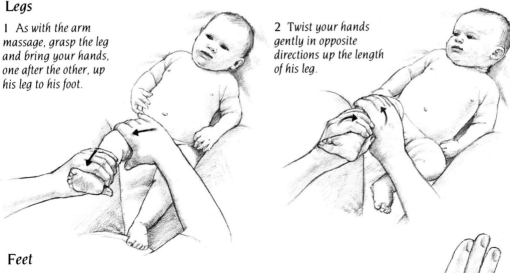

Feet

1 As with his hands, massage the soles of his feet with both your thumbs, moving from heel to toe.

2 Next massage the sole in the same direction, but this time with the palm of your hand.

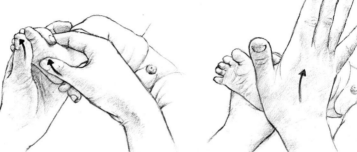

Back

1 (Above left) Place him across you on your outstretched legs or on a cushion. Massage slowly down his back, moving your hands in opposite directions across his back. Carry on using a steady, regular rhythm, until you have covered the length of his spine.

2 (Above right) Shift him to your right so he is almost kneeling on the floor. Support his bottom with your right hand and stroke down the length of his spine with your left hand.
3 (Right) With his feet in your right hand, massage all the way down to his heels.

Face

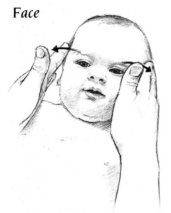

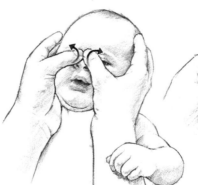

1 Gently draw your finger tips away from the center of his forehead and move them outwards along his eyebrows. Bring them back to the center and repeat the movement.

2 With your thumbs on each side of the bridge of his nose, move them both lightly together up the sides towards his forehead. Repeat the movement.

3 Move your thumbs lightly down over his eyelids. Continue along either side of his nose and then down to the corners of his mouth; gently stretching them out. Repeat the movement.

Soothing . . . .

If your baby is overtired or agitated and unable to sleep or feed, it's important to be able to soothe her. The noise she is making and the thrashing movements of her arms and legs will make it difficult for her to attend to anything else, but if you hold her closely and talk to her quietly, this may be enough to calm her. If not, you can try some of the alternatives described below.

Singing to your baby as you gently rock him will often help to soothe him.

Swaddling your baby

Wrapping her securely, but not tightly, when she's ready for sleep, will stop her from being disturbed by her own movements. The way of swaddling described below is one that you may like to develop to suit your own baby.

2 Wrap the upper part of the short end of the cloth over her right arm. Tuck it under the arm, following the direction of the arrow.

3 Take the bottom corner of the short end and bring it up and over her body so she is covered from the waist downwards. Tuck the edge in firmly underneath her body as shown.

4 Wrap the upper long end of the cloth over her left arm and tuck it in firmly underneath.

5 Take the bottom corner of the long end up and across her body so the top edge falls across her right shoulder.

6 Fold the loose end of the cloth underneath her and out to the other side. Keep the top edge of the cloth at the level of her neck.

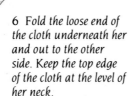

7 Bring the free end of the cloth around across the front of her body and secure it with a safety pin.

Swaddling

In the first few weeks of life, your baby may find it comforting to be closely wrapped in a shawl or crib sheet before being settled to sleep. In this way she will not be disturbed by the random movements of her own limbs and at the same time she may find reassurance and a sense of security similar to that which she experienced in the womb.

Two of my own babies were born in a country where swaddling was common practice and for the first few weeks I followed the local custom and found it very effective – my babies appearing noticeably calmer and more contented when swaddled. In fact, research has now shown that swaddled babies sleep more, cry less and spend more of their waking time actively alert than other babies[23].

Carriers

In many parts of Africa and China, babies spend a good deal of their time wrapped closely in a shawl tied securely to their mothers' bodies. The close physical contact and constant movement make for very contented babies who rarely cry. In the developed world, a growing awareness of the soothing effects of baby carriers has led to their general availability in a wide variety of forms, enabling mothers to carry their babies in a similarly close and secure fashion.

Choosing a carrier

Consider the following points when you choose a carrier: Does it provide adequate support for a young baby's head? Will it expand to accommodate a growing baby? Is it easy to put on without help?

Right This carrier has a detachable head rest, padded seat and straps and expandable leg holes. It is easy to put on and fastens simply with a metal clip at the back.

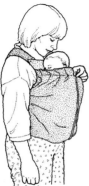

Left This is a pouch within a pouch, and the type of carrier that holds very small babies securely. Tucks at the neck can be loosened to make it adjustable for a growing baby. To put it on, you slip your arms through the shoulder straps and then tie the lower strings, like an apron, at the back.

Try to introduce your baby to a carrier from an early age as she may not take to it so easily at a later age. Once she can support her head, she will enjoy looking at her surroundings from this advantageous viewpoint. You will soon come to appreciate the ease with which you can carry her around the house. Out shopping or traveling on public transportation, the reassuring warmth and closeness of your body together with your movements will help to keep her happy. If she is agitated and you are using the carrier to soothe her, you will find that once she is asleep you can easily transfer her to her crib or carriage.

Sheepskins

Premature babies appear noticeably more contented when settled to sleep on a sheepskin. Indeed, many mothers have claimed that their babies go to sleep more easily with the added comfort and warmth of a fleece beneath them. Sheepskins can be used in cradles and buggies or on the floor and are very easy to wash.

Rhythmic sounds and movement

A baby listens to the sounds of her mother's heartbeat and breathing while in the womb, so it's not so surprising that after birth, sounds of a similar nature are likely to reassure and comfort her. While lying at her mother's breast, either when feeding or while being carried around in a carrier, she can feel her rhythmic breathing and this may help to soothe her to sleep. One can even buy tape recordings of the sounds a baby hears when inside the womb and these can help to calm a very young baby and settle her to sleep. Interestingly, two researchers working at home with their own young babies gave them the choice of listening to tapes of womb sounds, childrens' music or classical music and found that, to begin with, they showed a distinct preference for the womb sounds. However, they soon lost interest in this tape and began to show an obvious preference for the children's music[24].

Some mothers have found that the whirring sound of a vacuum cleaner helps to soothe a baby; others that a short trip in the car can have a magically soothing effect when every effort to calm a crying baby has failed. Possibly the reason that a loud, continuous sound like a car's motor quiets a baby is because it drowns the sound of her crying, and if she cannot hear herself cry, she may actually forget she's crying! Another technique which surprisingly also works, for possibly the same reason, involves seating your baby facing you on your lap and singing to her on one note, rather more loudly than her cries[25]. You'll notice her paying attention and if you quiet your singing, she may cease crying and become alert and attentive to the change in volume.

Babies enjoy rhythmic movement and you may find that you can calm a crying baby simply by holding her securely and rocking her rapidly with an up and down motion.

In a carrier your baby can sleep peacefully, lulled by the motion of your body, while you have both hands free to play with another child.

• COMMUNICATING •

Babies cannot communicate using language but they do manage to let you know about their needs, likes and dislikes from a very early age with the help of body movements, facial expressions and vocal exclamations. In fact, your baby is ready for social activity from birth, but at first much of your interaction will take place around feeding time or when she is being bathed or changed. As she starts to feed less frequently and sleep progressively less, you will both have more time for communicating. Remember that at this early stage, yours is by far the largest part in the communication and as she cannot yet give you a clear idea of what she wants, she will need you to act as interpreter.

Spending time with the family

Allowing her to spend more time with the rest of the family will encourage other adults to stop and talk to her. Everyone she meets has a slightly different way of relating to her and it's as well to get her used to a variety of styles and approaches. Visiting grandparents may love to spend time with her, playing games that they remember from looking after their own children. They may be especially sensitive and respond to her with just the right sounds and movements.

Other children

Other children can play an important part in your baby's life, as even in her first year they can show great sensitivity when communicating with her and also provide exciting stimulation. I remember the rides my own ten-year-old gave to his new brother, zooming him round the room at shoulder height like an airplane, taking great care of him but playing in a way that would never have occurred to me.

It's a good idea to encourage an elder brother or sister, even if only a toddler, to help with a new baby right from the start and to play and talk with her. Research has shown that where this is encouraged, a good relationship develops between the child and baby[26]. Try to involve your other children as much as possible in the time you spend with your baby to prevent them from feeling jealous. You can help them to feel wanted and needed by asking them to pass you some powder or a clean diaper as you are changing the baby or by encouraging them to help you choose which clothes the baby will wear the next day. In this way, they will come to care for her and share your concern for her well-being.

Attracting your attention . . . .

As a parent it may seem only natural to you that you should find your baby beautiful in the way she looks and moves. In reality, a baby's appearance – her large eyes and forehead, tiny nose and

Crying

A toddler will have her own special ways of communicating with a baby, touching her gently, showing her a favorite toy, talking to her all the while.

later her toddling walk — evokes feelings of tenderness and protection in other human beings and is one of the more subtle ways she has of attracting your attention and ensuring that you continue to care for her.

Your newborn baby soon learns that crying is the most effective way of attracting your attention. She does not understand the effect her crying is having on you but she knows that it is usually rewarded by your attention. By associating crying with your presence, she is beginning to have an idea of the effect she can have on you. In fact, crying can be seen as one of her first steps towards communicating with a purpose.

She may cry because she is hungry, uncomfortable or in pain, or because she is overtired, upset or bored. Each cry is distinctive and with its own particular message, and although you may not consciously distinguish one from another, you may find yourself instinctively reacting differently in each case. Even when still in the hospital, mothers quickly come to recognize the message behind their babies' different cries, and there is no reason to suspect that fathers are any less discriminating once they get to know their babies.

Don't be afraid of spoiling your baby by going to her when she cries. Giving her attention when she asks for it, especially in the early months, is not going to make her spoiled or over-demanding.

Early smiles

At some time around two months, babies find a new and delightful way of attracting your attention and engaging you in conversation and play – they start to smile. You may think you have caught your baby smiling earlier than this but this was probably more in response to feelings inside her own body than to anything happening in the world outside. For example, she may have given you a recognizably 'gassy' smile in response to movements she felt in her digestive system.

Babies often show great pleasure and excitement when brothers or sisters stop to chat and play with them. In her second month, this baby gives her brother one of her very first smiles.

At around six to eight weeks, the mere sight of a human face may be enough to make your baby smile. Research has shown that it is the eyes more than any other feature of the human face which

cause a baby to smile[27]. Even if the lower part of the face is covered, the baby will still smile so long as she can see both eyes; interestingly, profiles of a face showing only one eye have no effect. Most surprising of all is the discovery that a baby of this age will smile at a mask with two black ovals in the place of eyes, even if it contains no other recognizable features.

'Conversations' . . . .

Listen to a mother talking to her baby and you will notice that she behaves as if the baby is already capable of communicating. She asks questions and then pauses, waiting for the baby's answers before going on to supply them herself. She lets her baby set the pace, waiting for her to finish sucking before she starts to speak and then gently responding to the small noises the baby makes as if they were words. In this way, the mother is giving her baby a message of positive encouragement, showing her that she understands and that her message is getting through.

This way of talking to babies comes naturally to most people. If you are a mother or father who is not naturally talkative, you may feel self-conscious at first, but try it once and your baby's attentive look will encourage you to carry on. Remember that she is listening to everything you say even though she cannot understand the sense of what you are saying and that she will soon become sensitive to the tone of your voice, your mood and eventually the message you are trying to get across. By listening to you and by taking her part in these 'conversations', she will finally come to express herself and to understand others.

When you talk to your baby, you will find yourself quite naturally speaking gently and slower and more deliberately than usual, using a higher tone and lots of repetition and questions tagged onto the end of sentences in the following way ". . . you like it, don't you?" or ". . . it's nice and warm, isn't it?" Any subject is suitable for conversation: "Mommy's gone out in the car . . .yes she has, hasn't she? . . she's gone to see Auntie Jane . . . yes, in the car . . . hasn't she?" and so on. Whatever you choose to tell her, your baby will listen intently, concentrating on your face and voice. You can talk about what you are doing to her as you change and dress her and then discuss where you are going to take her that afternoon. She for her part will gaze into your face, watching and listening attentively, and occasionally taking her turn in the conversation. Many psychologists believe that it is experiences like these that teach your baby one of the most important rules of human communication – to take turns[28]. It is something your baby will pick up quickly so that as you talk, she quiets, as if waiting for you to finish before she takes her turn.

SMILES
AND LAUGHTER
· ·
AROUND 3 MONTHS

Introduction ....

Your baby makes obvious progress at around three months. He sleeps less now and more regularly – three or four times every 24 hours – and you'll probably find that he's beginning to adapt to your rhythm, sleeping more during the night and less during the day. When he's awake, he spends less of his time crying.

The more time he spends alert and responsive, the more chance you will have to get to know him. He's starting to emerge as an individual in his own right with a distinctive personality and temperament, which is bound to affect the type of games you play with him. A quiet baby may prefer gentle games engaging his sight and hearing whereas an active baby may prefer more boisterous, physical play. Whatever his temperament, he's rewarding company, responsive and friendly both to those he knows and to strangers, and his smiles and laughter make every game and 'conversation' that much more enjoyable.

Most noticeable during these first few months is the marked interest he shows in novelty – preferring experiences, objects and events that are different, but not too different, from those he has met before. If he sees or hears something that is too different from an earlier experience, he is unable to deal with it and so pays it no attention. On the other hand, if an experience is too familiar, it no longer holds his attention. He has mastered all it can offer him for

A baby may seem to take the lead when 'talking' to her mother but it's difficult to know who's imitating whom. Together they build up a pattern of facial expressions and sounds – open mouthed 'aahs' (left), pursed lipped 'oohs' (center right) and finally laughter (right).

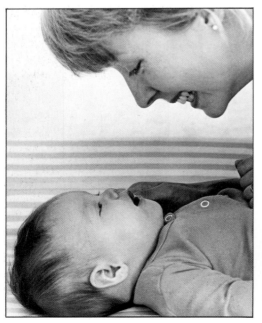 

the moment and so has no further use for it. If you bear this in mind during the games you play together, you will more readily pick up the signals he gives you when he has had enough of a particular game or when he is ready for you to introduce some new variation.

•ACQUIRING PHYSICAL SKILLS•

Changes are taking place in your baby's central nervous system as higher levels of the brain start to come into use. Both the grasping and Moro reflexes disappear about now, and it's exciting to watch him as he starts to develop control over his own movements. He's becoming noticeably more co-ordinated and has growing strength in important muscles in his neck and shoulders.

Holding up his head

As his muscles gain in strength, he is able to hold up his head for longer and longer periods without your support. If you hold him seated on your lap or up against your shoulder, you'll notice him watching people, turning both his eyes and head to follow their movements. Sometimes he'll throw back his head to get a different view of the world and laugh with delight at his changed perspective. He enjoys being able to change his viewpoint quite dramatically in this way and may repeat the action frequently, laughing every time.

 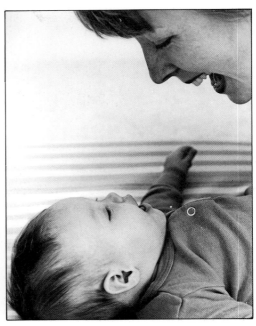

From now on, you can carry him in a baby sling or carrier without a head support. He has a much wider field of vision and is now able to focus on objects at a distance so he'll enjoy being taken for walks, carried in this way.

On his tummy

If you place him lying on his tummy, you'll see that he now has enough strength to lift both his head and shoulders from the floor. Most babies love to lie in this way if they are introduced to it from an early age and I have found that if a baby is fussing or crying, placing him in this position may help to distract or soothe him. Raised on his forearms, he can view and join in everything going on around him.

You can give her the chance to try out her developing strength by placing soft foam blocks at the bottom of her basket for her to kick against. Some contain bells which jingle when she kicks them.

Keep a rug and toys with you in the part of the house in which you spend most of your time so you can settle him in this position quickly and easily. He will love to gaze at other children playing on the floor in front of him, but take care to place him at a safe distance. He will find it even more enjoyable if you get down on the floor beside him so that you are on his level for talking and playing with him. Your baby may be reluctant to lie on his front at first, but you can help him adapt to it by following the method illustrated below.

Lying your baby on his tummy

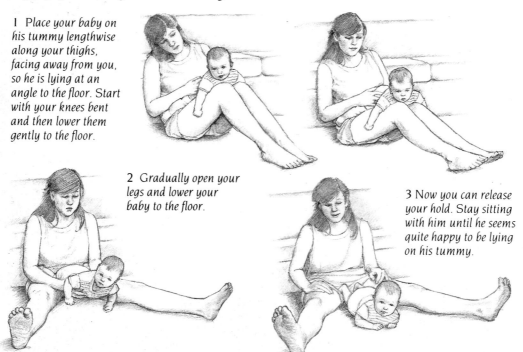

1 Place your baby on his tummy lengthwise along your thighs, facing away from you, so he is lying at an angle to the floor. Start with your knees bent and then lower them gently to the floor.

2 Gradually open your legs and lower your baby to the floor.

3 Now you can release your hold. Stay sitting with him until he seems quite happy to be lying on his tummy.

Turning his head

You can vary the rattle game you played earlier so that it gives him the opportunity to exercise his developing neck muscles (see page 30). Stand behind him when he's lying on his back so that he concentrates on the rattle and not on you. Then move it in a big circle round his head, first clockwise and then counter-clockwise, or move it in a semi-circle from one side of his head to the other at a distance of about 15 cm (12 in). As long as you move it at a speed at which he can keep track of it, you'll notice him moving both his head and eyes to follow its movements. He'll quite happily play the same game when he's lying on his tummy supporting himself on his forearms. Remember that however much he appears to enjoy this game, it involves a lot of effort on his part so take care not to overtire him.

Kicking and bouncing

Lying him on his back on your thighs with his feet towards your stomach is another position he enjoys, particularly if you let him use his developing strength to push against your body with his feet. He loves to use his feet in this way, so you can try putting soft toys or fabric blocks at the bottom of his crib for him to kick against. A bag filled with crinkly paper is something else he can enjoy as it will make an intriguing rustling noise when he kicks against it.

He enjoys trying his feet on the ground, too. When his legs are long enough, you can sit him astride your thigh, letting his feet touch the ground so they take some of his weight. Then, supporting him under his arms, bounce him gently up and down. Soon he'll start to flex his knees as he pushes himself up from the floor. As the weeks go by and he gains greater control over his trunk, you can gradually lower the position of your hands on his body.

Introducing him to water . . . .

We now know that given the chance, very young babies can learn to swim before they can walk, and Russian experiments have produced photographic evidence of babies swimming unassisted both above and below the surface[29]! However, you will need to introduce your baby gently to water and it will take time and patience on your part, perhaps with the guidance of a teacher, to get him to the stage where he will feel confident enough to swim in armbands with you close by, but no longer supporting him. It's a good idea to introduce him to water early on as he may not take to it so easily at a later age, but you should not consider taking him to a public pool until he has had at least two sets of immunizations. The water in public pools is too cold and the chlorine too strong for very young babies. By the age of six months, though, you should be able to start him in a program for "water babies" at your local Y. For now he can play in the bath with you firmly supporting him.

Fascinated by the sight and sound of a rattle as it moves, a baby will turn her head to follow it with her eyes. As you move it over her head in an arc, she may only follow it halfway to begin with.

Enjoying bathtime

Bathtime provides all sorts of opportunities for play, involving your baby's senses at every level. He experiences different sensations of touch – wet and dry skin, changes in temperature, the firm, smooth feel of your hands soaping him and the soft friction of the towel as you dry him. He'll also enjoy the noises of dripping and splashing water and the gurgle of pipes.

Water in itself provides novel enjoyment for a young baby. It moves, catching the light. It resists touch less than solid things, but more than air, so movement in it and through it feels different. And as long as your baby has your support, he is free to move his limbs in a variety of ways and can kick and splash vigorously. You can join in his play in various ways – gently splashing, trickling water on his body and moving him through the water. It's best to avoid anything too sudden or boisterous, and not to repeat anything he appears unsure of. A gentle and gradual approach to new games will help to build his confidence so that he grows up unafraid of water.

Sharing your bath

A further range of possibilities opens up if you sometimes share your bath with your baby. Because you're with him, supporting him firmly in the water, you can run the bath deeper than when he's alone, and join in his play. Apart from play, sharing your bath makes for close physical contact between you. You may especially appreciate this if you are a father, or a mother who is not breast-feeding.

Bathtime becomes so much more fun when it's shared with someone else – quiet moments of close contact can follow moments of more active play.

Holding him in an upright position will give him greater freedom for kicking and splashing. You can also get him used to floating on his back with your hands firmly supporting him.

SAFETY AND COMFORT IN THE BATH

- Pour the cold water first and then the hot to prevent the bottom of the bath from getting too hot

- Test the temperature of the water with your elbow before putting the baby into the bath. Make sure it is a comfortable temperature for him – you may be used to much hotter water but this would not be safe for him

- Long sessions in the bath are not a good idea as the water may go cold and your baby will quickly become chilled

- When you wash your baby, hold him securely as soap will make both your hands and his skin very slippery

- If you share a bath with your baby, place a non-slip rubber mat on the bottom of the bath to prevent you from slipping or sliding as you wash and play with him

- If you are in the bath with your baby, make sure there is another adult within earshot to lift him in and out. Don't try lifting him out yourself as it's far too easy to slip when doing so

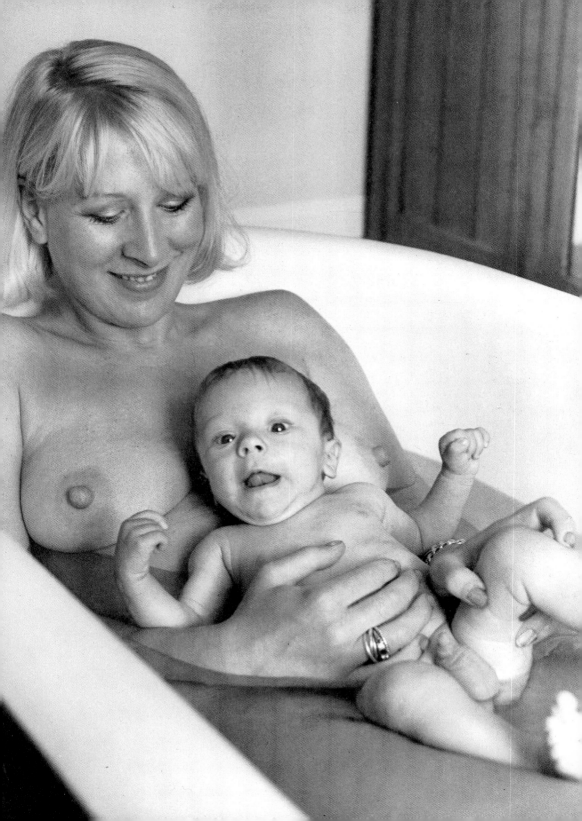

• PERCEIVING THE WORLD •

Your baby is more often awake and alert now and better able to perceive and enjoy his surroundings. He can see just about as well as an adult, and his hearing and other senses are almost fully developed. Now is a wonderful time for introducing him to the richness of the world around him, especially if you try to see it all through his eyes and imagine how each new experience must feel to him.

Show him large shiny mirrors and lampshades. Let him get to know the feel of different textures: stroke a soft cotton puff over his hand and follow it with the smooth surface of a baby brush. Keep him with you in the kitchen when you're preparing meals so that he can smell the rich and varied scents of different foods. Sing and talk to him and let him listen closely to the sound of a clock ticking or a refrigerator humming. Dance with him to your favorite music or rock him gently in your arms. Take him out of doors where he can feel the change in temperature and the contrast in light as you walk from shadow to sunlight. During these and all your other activities together, he is busy absorbing his environment, interpreting all the messages he receives in order to make sense of his surroundings.

Seeing . . . .

During his first few months, your baby concentrated visually on placing things in his environment. Now he's becoming interested in the different shapes and colors of the patterns that the outlines contain. More complex patterns are starting to hold his attention, and research has shown that during the first year a baby shows a definite preference for shapes that are circular and curved[30].

Any pattern you draw for him can be fixed to the wall within his view or hung over his crib. Remember that he has plenty of natural

What your baby likes to look at

Circular patterns
Distinct outlines and circular shapes catch his attention.

You can draw spirals and bull's-eyes and hang them in his crib.

Faces
Black dots for eyes and a smiling mouth make a human face.

Add some hair and make a cuddly padded toy.

patterns around him to choose from. He may be intrigued by the bars of his crib, the criss cross pattern on his blanket or the stripes on his sleeper. If you place his stroller under a tree in the garden, the gentle movement of the leaves and the constantly changing patterns of light may catch his eye and keep him entertained for quite some time.

Faces

It is no longer just the features of your face which interest him, but its pattern as a whole. He's beginning to memorize the different patterns of people's faces and can recognize a familiar face by sight alone – he no longer needs to hear a voice as well[31]. And he may even signal his recognition with a smile!

You may well have noticed a puzzled or worried look on his face if you suddenly appear within his sight wearing a bath towel on your head or a new pair of dark glasses. This is because he has studied your face carefully, forming a very clear idea of it in his own mind, and any change is bound to leave him bewildered. He will need to be reassured that you are still the same person underneath that bath towel or behind those dark glasses!

In response to his fascination for faces, you can draw a round or oval face with well-marked features on a piece of cardboard or wood or cloth and hang it near the crib or stick it to the bars of the crib. If you decide to use cloth, you can stuff or pad it so your baby can use it as a soft toy later on. In this case, it's a good idea for both the stuffing and cloth to be washable, and very important for the features and hair to be securely sewn on as a young baby can easily choke on a button or a loose strand of wool.

OBJECT CONSTANCY

Research has shown that by this time your baby will realize that objects keep their identity even though certain aspects of their appearance may change[32]. Adults take this ability for granted but for a baby it involves the following realizations:

- that an object retains its identity even though its color may appear lighter or darker depending on whether it is seen in bright light or shadow

- that an object retains its identity even though it appears larger or smaller depending on how near or far away it is

- that an object retains its identiy even though it may appear different depending on the angle from which it is seen and that this angle may change constantly if the object or observer is in motion

Touch . . . .

At two or three months, he will hold onto a rattle if it is placed in his hand, and may cry if he loses it. He doesn't yet quite know how to go about getting things for himself but is fascinated by anything moving and will reach out to grasp it. Reaching out brings his own hand to his attention and you'll notice how, again and again, he stops, distracted from what he is trying to do by the sight of it.

He loves to play with his hands at this stage, investigating them thoroughly – feeling them all over, grasping and pulling at his fingers. He holds them up above his face, making further discoveries about the way they look and feel. It's lovely to watch a baby totally absorbed in this type of spontaneous play, seemingly oblivious to anything else going on around him.

For the moment, this fascination with his hands prevents him from using them to grasp hold of things he can see. To help make up for this, you can place toys for him to grasp where he is likely to find them by touch alone. He drops things frequently at this stage, especially if he catches sight of them, so it's a good idea to string any toys across his crib where he can easily find them again by touch. Or play with him by giving him a variety of rattles to hold, one after another, making sure they are the right size and shape for his tiny grasp. When choosing a rattle, remember that he will enjoy feeling its texture and shape as well as looking at its bright colors and listening to the noise it makes.

Rattles

Whether you decide to buy or make your own, remember that what your baby enjoys about a rattle is the way it looks, moves and feels and the particular sound it makes.

Traditional shape
Basket work is light and has an interesting feel to it

Dumbell
Easy to hold by its narrow middle. Sharp rattle sound

Ball
Holes for fingers to grip, and a bell to ring

Ring
Wide enough to hold with both hands. Colored balls whizz around inside

Cage
Spaces for small fingers and a bell to ring inside

Ring of beads
Distinctive click as the beads knock together

String of triangles
When shaken makes an intriguing clattering sound

He stares fixedly at a rattle held in front of him (*top*). But when placed in his grasp (*middle*), a look of intense concentration comes over his face as he tries to keep hold of it (*bottom*).

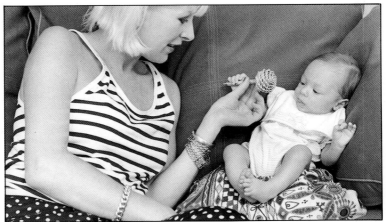

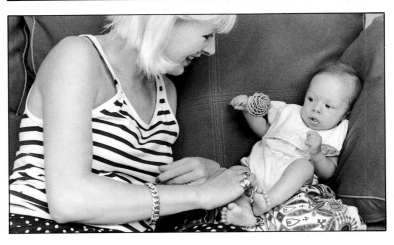

• COMMUNICATING •

The time your baby spends with you is very important to him as you offer him such a wide variety of different behavior to observe and learn from. He still prefers experiences that are different, but not too different, from those he has met before, and your behavior provides the ideal combination. Your actions are never totally predictable and yet he can trust you to act with his interests in mind, taking care not to tire or bewilder him with too much stimulation.

This mutual understanding comes about during the first couple of months through the many intimate moments you have shared together. You have become more attuned to how he responds – the different qualities of his cries and what they mean, how he turns his head away when he's had enough of a game and how he signals fear if excitement begins to grow into panic. He has come to anticipate your reactions – soothing him when he cries and responding to his engaging ways with talk and games.

Smiling and laughing

Babies vary greatly as to when they first start to smile, and there is little you can do to make your baby smile before he is ready to do so – some are real smilers at only seven weeks, others do not smile until they are ten or twelve weeks old. There is some evidence, however, that serious lack of intimacy and familiarity with a

---

TOYS AND SAFETY

Many toys, especially those produced by the larger, well-established manufacturers, are designed to meet stringent safety regulations. However, unsafe toys do appear on the market and there are various hazards to watch out for with home-made toys.

- Make sure that the toy contains no small parts which can come loose and be swallowed

- Avoid toys with holes small enough to trap a baby's fingers

- Avoid toys with sharp or splintery edges and those made out of fragile plastic or other material which breaks easily and leaves sharp edges

- Avoid toys that are hard or heavy enough to be painful if dropped on toes or fingers.

- Make sure that the material from which the toy is made is non-toxic and non-inflammable

- Avoid rattles and teethers which have any part narrow and long enough to reach to the back of a baby's mouth

- Avoid long strings which can be swallowed or which may become wrapped around a baby's neck

- Inspect all home-made toys regularly for any new cracks or breakages which could be harmful

caregiver can delay a baby's first smile. Studies of children brought up in institutions have shown that they tend to smile rather later and less often than other children, probably because they have less contact with their caregivers and are less rewarded by their attention when they do smile[33].

Most people are won over by a smiling baby. You must have experienced your own baby holding your gaze with his own and smiling in such a way that there is little you can do but respond by playing and talking with him. At other times, it may have been you who took the initiative, coaxing him to smile for you. By now your eyes are no longer enough to make him smile, he likes to see your nose and mouth and soon your whole face. In return, he will smile with his eyes and they'll crinkle up when he sees you. He smiles more frequently every day: when you pick him up for his feeding, when you talk to him and when you play with him.

We now know for certain that such smiles are not just imitations of adult smiles, as blind children smile in response to touch and the sound of human voices without ever having seen a human face, although they do so at a much later age than children who can see[34]. So you can rest assured that your baby's smile is a clear indication that he's feeling good inside himself.

Shortly after he starts to smile, he will start to laugh, usually at something unexpected, particularly if it turns out to be not as threatening as it may have seemed at first. If you suddenly move your head towards him in play, for example, he may look startled at first and then laugh with relief when he realizes your playful intentions.

Using his voice

He's experimenting with another type of behavior that is destined to attract and hold your attention and encourage your attempts to communicate with him. He's beginning to make sounds that are much closer to the sounds used in adult speech.

When he's feeling contented, he makes soft cooing noises. At other times, he squeals and gurgles with pleasure and can be quite earsplitting in his delight. He's also experimenting with his newly discovered ability to stop and alter the flow of sound he's making by constricting the muscles at the back of his mouth. In this way he starts to add guttural consonants like 'k' and 'g' to the sounds he's making. He's also less tactful than when he was younger about taking turns in the conversations he has with others. In fact, he far prefers to join in a chorus with you when you talk to him, adding to the noise level with great enjoyment. Even when alone in his crib, he loves to practice the many different sounds in his repertoire and thoroughly enjoys the sound of his own voice.

Encouraging communication

'Conversations' and games together are really enjoyable at this stage. He loves playing with you because you are continually

Physical play is a special delight and provides a baby with information about the way her body moves. Here a baby is enjoying her father's own particular style of boisterous play.

responsive to him in a way toys cannot be. In fact, at this stage his interest in toys is limited to the times when you pick them up and make them move for him. He enjoys his time with you, the ways in which he can get a response from you and the ingenuity of your games.

It's fascinating to watch an adult engrossed in play with a baby of this age, attentive to all his smallest signals, building up his expectations and making sure the sequence ends in a climax. One such game can be played when he's lying in his stroller. You can rock it gently so that it makes its characteristic squeak, timing your movements and counting aloud "one . . . two . . . three", building up to a climax as you finish the game with a "shake rattle and roll". You'll notice him holding his breath in anticipation for the final climax. When you sense he may be getting bored with one ending, add a final twist "one . . . two . . . . three . . . . . tickle him on his tummy".

The games you play can involve all the baby's different senses — making use of words repeated at different tempos; whispering close to his ear imitations of the sounds he makes; blowing spluttery raspberries on his tummy or neck; walking your fingers slowly up his body and ending with a light touch on his nose, or trickling water gently and rhythmically on his tummy in the bath.

You can sit him on your knee and clap different rhythms with his hands, maybe singing as you go, or place his arms by his sides and lift them up and out and then down again as if they were wings — making bird sounds as you do so. If you lie him on his back and let him push against your hands with his feet and then gradually start to bicycle his legs round and round, he will enjoy experiencing the different ways in which his legs can move.

He also likes to listen to you as you build up a pattern of sound, clicking your tongue and popping your lips, especially if you alter the sounds to suit his rhythm. He'll particularly enjoy it if you introduce small crescendos and surprise sounds from time to time. The possibilities are endless and other games are bound to come to mind as you play with him.

. . . .

NEW
HORIZONS
· · · · · · · · · · ·
4-7 MONTHS

Introduction . . . .

Your baby is beginning to see life from quite another angle. Not only is she now able to sit up and look around her, she also has greater control over her own movements, and the way in which her nervous system is developing means that she can deal with more complicated tasks. The possibilities for play expand wonderfully in line with her rapidly developing physical abilities and mental awareness, making this an exciting and enjoyable time for all concerned.

She's also beginning to make sense of all the information accumulated over the past months and is making important discoveries about the nature of people, things and events. To some extent she has played her own part in all this by actively searching for information, but the breadth of her experience has been largely in your hands. This is why the time she spends with you and others is so important – it provides her with the variety of experience she needs to form a coherent picture of the world around her.

What may strike you most at this age is that she is such a happy individual, contented and enjoying life, happy to greet and play with friends and newcomers alike. In fact, this is an ideal time for introducing her to others who may help to look after her in the future – whether babysitters, relatives or friends – as she has not yet reached the age where shyness and fear of strangers will make her reserved and less easy to get to know.

Sitting up

Below At four months she can sit if you support her under her arms but will topple over if you release your hold.

Below At seven months she can sit alone and unsupported – a sign of growing independence.

Above At five or six months she can balance in a sitting position but still needs support at waist level.

· ACQUIRING PHYSICAL SKILLS ·

Much of what your baby has been trying to achieve in the last month materializes about now. During this period she learns to sit up unsupported, to reach out and grasp hold of the object she desires and to change her position by rolling over. These developments mean that not only is she gaining control over her own body, but she is also better able to control what is happening around her.

Sitting up

As her spine becomes stronger and she gains control over increasingly more of the upper part of her body, she will need less support when sitting up. Seated on your knee at around four months, she will still need you to support her under her arms but, as the weeks progress, you can gradually lower the position of your hands, first to her waist and eventually to her hips. By about six months, she'll be able to sit upright in a chair without slumping, and by seven months, she should be able to sit unsupported on the ground, although she may need a few cushions behind and to the side of her to begin with to soften the fall if she keels over. She no longer needs her hands and arms for support and so is free to use them for exploring and playing with objects around her.

You may have an infant seat to which you can attach a tray; if not, now is a good time to get one. She'll enjoy playing with toys on the tray for short periods as a change from being on the floor and, once she's eating solid foods, she can use it for meals as well. A

Baby chairs

Infant seats
An easy chair/car seat (see page 36) can now be adjusted to a semi-upright position (below left). A reclining infant seat (see page 36) can be placed in an upright position and a tray attached for eating and playing (below right).

High chairs
A high chair comes in useful now as it puts her on your level. You can chat to her while she eats or plays with her toys on a tray.

safety harness is, of course, essential and she should never be left in a chair without one at this stage. Alternatively, putting her in a high chair gives her the novel experience of being on a level with the rest of the family and means that she can join them at table where there is plenty for her to see and hear. You can attach toys to her infant seat or high chair by suction. Some will bounce back on a spring when she hits them. They may also have a transparent globe so she can see the movement of the small figures or balls that whirl about inside.

Co-ordinating hands and eyes

She's recently been able to pinpoint an object of interest with her eyes or to reach out for it with her hands, but she hasn't yet been able to combine the two. During her fifth month, she's suddenly able to co-ordinate looking and grasping. When looking at an object which she finds attractive, she'll reach out with one hand, leaning forward from a sitting position so she almost folds in two at the waist, and, keeping her eyes fixed firmly on the object, grasp hold of it triumphantly.

She rapidly becomes more and more adept at using her hands. If

A readiness to share in her baby brother's sense of achievement, as he reaches out and success-fully grabs hold of a toy, will encourage him to try other demanding feats.

you give her a toy such as a small ball to hold, she will curl her fingers and thumb around it, clasping it to her palm. To begin with, her hold on things is fairly precarious and if she wants to hold something securely she must grasp it with both hands or clasp it to her chest with one hand.

She finds your hair irresistible at this stage and as she can't yet let go of things at will, you may find yourself constantly disentangling your hair from her fingers, only to find that she then tries to grab hold of your nose or some other part of your face!

This success in reaching and grasping is partly due to the fact that her hands are losing the totally absorbing fascination they have held for her over the past weeks: she's found out all she can learn from them for the moment and is no longer interested in exploring their appearance and feel. She's now far more interested in what they can do.

Now that she can get hold of some of the things she wants and investigate them thoroughly, you can give her a variety of objects of different shapes and sizes to play with – jello molds, baking pans and empty spools of thread. Remember that everything that comes into her grasp goes straight to her mouth (see page 78), so make sure that any object you give her to play with is too large to be swallowed.

Falling objects

She's only just mastered the skill of grasping, so she frequently lets objects drop at this stage without meaning to. To begin with, she may show some surprise each time she loses her grip in this way, but she'll enjoy watching the way objects fall and roll in different ways – metal objects that clatter to the floor, soft toys that fall quietly and handkerchiefs that float gently away.

Learning about lifting

Experiments have shown that a baby will actually tense the muscles of her hand and arm as she prepares herself to lift objects of different weights. Past experience has already given her expectations about the weight of different things, and she's starting to judge from their appearance how much effort she needs to make to pick them up. However, if you give her an object to hold which is lighter than it looks, she'll be unprepared and her hand will shoot up in compensation.

She'll pick up quite a wide range of objects of different sizes and weights that come to hand. Small bean bags are interesting objects for her to handle – floppy and graspable as the beans shift about inside the bag. You can make her a selection of bean bags of different weights to hold, simply by filling small cloth bags of varying sizes with dried beans and sewing the ends securely.

From hand to hand

At four months, if she's holding a cube and you hand her another, she drops the first one automatically to open her hand for the second. At around seven months, she acquires the knack of transferring things from one hand to the other, and will transfer the cube she is holding into her free hand before taking the second cube with her other hand. At this stage, she enjoys playing with lightweight toys such as plastic or wooden rings, or small soft toys, which you can make out of terry cloth and fill with some washable material. A flat "gingerbread man" is very simple to make, and the arms and legs are easy for her to grasp hold of – a bell sewn inside will make an interesting, muffled sound as she shakes it around. Rattles are also very popular at this stage, and you can easily make your own by filling small, clean plastic bottles with a few lentils. Different objects, such as marbles, rice or dry spaghetti, make a variety of sounds when placed in different shaped bottles, and, as long as you screw the tops on tightly, they are perfectly safe for her to play with.

Investigating things by mouth

Hands, eyes and ears are not the only means your baby has for finding out about the objects that come into her grasp. Her mouth is highly sensitive and richly endowed with sensory receptors that are very effective at picking up information about the taste, texture, shape and hardness or softness of objects. Everything she picks up will go straight to her mouth for investigation. Only when she has explored an object carefully with her mouth, felt it with her tongue and chewed on it with her gums, does she really feel that she knows what it's about.

In fact, a baby's mouth is so effective at learning about the qualities of objects that she can recognize an object by sight after getting to know it with her mouth, even though she has never seen it. Experiments have shown that babies who were given differently shaped pacifiers to suck recognized them later by sight, even though they had not been allowed to see them [35].

One of the objects your baby successfully grabs hold of at this time is her own foot, which she handles and looks at and then puts

---

TOYS AND SAFETY

- Do not let her play with plastic bags. If she should get one over her head, she could suffocate

- Don't allow her to play with cracked or broken plastic cartons, as the sharp edges can cut her face or mouth

- Don't give her objects to play with that contain dye which may run or rub off – the dye from tissue paper runs and can be harmful, and the ink used in newspapers is toxic and rubs off easily

- Don't leave her playing with wrapping paper unattended, as small pieces break off when wet and need to be retrieved from her mouth at intervals

- Don't give her objects to play with that have long pieces of string attached, as she can suck and swallow the string

Toys and playthings

Everything is handled and mouthed at this stage, so she will particularly enjoy toys that have an interesting texture and feel to them. There are a wide variety you can buy, but many of them can be simply adapted from household objects.

She's also fascinated by toys that make a noise, and you can easily make these by filling containers with different objects to produce a variety of sounds. If you use clear containers, she can see the contents as she shakes them.

Hand toys

Firm rubbery fruit shapes

Smooth, hard plastic rings

A wooden ring threaded with interesting shapes

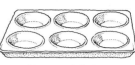

Cold, smooth baking pans and trays

Contents shift and slide to change the shapes of floppy bean bags

Different shaped hollows in a soft plastic ball for small hands to clutch

Light, plastic jello mold animals with noses, ears and toes to feel

Stuffed "gingerbread man" – soft and light for grasping, shaking and waving

Noise toys

Lentils rustle

Strands of broken spaghetti clatter

A squeaky squeezy monkey

Spoons and lids crash and bang against metal pots and pans

Marbles knock gently together

Dried beans rattle in a tin

Wooden beads make a satisfying clonk in a slotted cylinder

Tiny beads inside colored balls make a lovely musical sound

Mouth toys

Tough plastic cups and bowls

Funnels and measuring spoons

Rubber shapes squeak when chewed

Wooden and hard plastic napkin rings

Cool teething rings soothe sore gums

Firmly stuffed animals with chewable legs, noses and ears

into her mouth for further exploration. As she chews at her own toes, she gets to know not only their feel and taste but also the varying sensations that her chewing provokes. This is one of the ways she comes to learn about her own body and to realize that its various parts belong to her and are under her control.

If you look around the house, you're bound to come across suitable objects for her to mouth. Remember that whatever you give her should be unbreakable, too large to swallow, with no sharp edges or parts which come off, and no part narrow and long enough to reach to the back of her throat. Solid plastic cups and saucers, napkin rings in wood or hard plastic, empty salt shakers, kitchen funnels and measuring spoons are all suitable for chewing.

Many toys are also satisfactory for mouthing, so look out for different textures and shapes: terry cloth toys, squeaky squeezy plastic animals, hard silver teething rings – the sort that babies are often given for presents – wooden rattles and plastic shapes threaded securely on chains or strong nylon string. There are also a range of teething rings that can be put in the fridge to provide a cool surface for inflamed gums.

If you are with her, you can let her handle and chew on the spoon you feed her with, but don't leave her alone with it at this stage as she might push the end down her throat. Round about this age the first tooth appears and she starts to chew with her gums, so give her food she can handle herself, such as zwieback, crusts of bread, lengths of raw carrot or segments of firm apple. But don't leave her alone with food yet.

Banging and splashing

As the months go by, you'll find she loves to make a noise with her hands, banging on the table or splashing in the bath, and she enjoys it all the more if you join in as well. Any toys you give her to play with will need to be tough enough to withstand frequent bashings against the wall or floor, or whatever surface is within reach. As a change from some of the louder noises that her toys make as she shakes and bangs them, she may enjoy the chance to listen to some quiet, gentle sounds from a musical rattle or music

---

SAFETY AND COMFORT IN A BABY BOUNCER

- Make sure that the hook from which you are going to hang the bouncer is fixed securely to the beam or door frame

- Only leave your baby in the bouncer for short periods of ten to fifteen minutes. You may be tempted to leave her in for longer periods if she appears to be enjoying herself, but you should not do so, as this can cause abnormally persistent stiffness to develop in her legs and feet

- Never leave her in the bouncer unsupervised

Rolling from tummy to back

*Once your baby is able to
lift her head from the
floor (left) . . .*

*. . . a shift of her head to one side (center)
alters her balance and pulls her over
on to her back (right).*

box. You may be able to get hold of a music box which she can operate herself by pulling a handle or string, but she'll need your help to begin with to get it going.

Rolling

Around about six months, she makes the exciting new discovery that she no longer has to stay in exactly the position you put her in. She often practices lifting the top part of her body – from her shoulders down to her tummy – off the floor, by resting her weight on her forearms, but her balance is rather precarious because her head is still large and heavy in proportion to the rest of her body. So moving her head to one side may knock her off balance and cause her to roll over on to her back. The first couple of times she does so she'll look quite surprised, but once she has the whole sequence of movements under her control, she'll repeat it whenever she wants to. From now on, you'll need to be aware that you can no longer put her down in one position and expect her to stay there. Although she can't actually move very far at this stage, you'll need to make sure that there are no tablecloths, electrical cords or other hazards dangling nearby when you put her down to play on the floor.

Bouncing

Most babies enjoy being given the opportunity to exercise their limbs. Baby bouncer harnesses or seats that can be securely hung from a beam or door frame provide some support for your baby's back as well as allowing her feet to touch the floor. However, you should wait until your baby can support her trunk – at about six months – before introducing her to a baby bouncer.

A spring incorporated into the bouncer's suspension causes it to bounce up and down as your baby pushes with her feet against the floor. She will enjoy the different view she gets of her surroundings as the bouncer twists a little each time she moves, and if you put a bag full of paper or a mound of dry sand under her feet, the noise of rustling paper as she kicks, or the feeling of give and take as she bounces up and down on the sand, will make the experience even more enjoyable. You can even put a bowl of warm water underneath her feet if you don't mind the mess on the kitchen floor – she will love the freedom it gives her to splash, and, if you add some bubble bath, she will have the extra enjoyment of creating new bubbles each time she splashes. Take care to use bubble bath that is made specially for babies, so that if any does get near her face, she won't suffer from stinging eyes.

Bathtime fun . . . .

She can only just sit up, so it's easiest for her to keep stable and upright if you only run a shallow bath. For the moment she'll just enjoy patting and splashing the surface of the water, but she'll love it if you play at emptying containers in the bath. It's an activity which will hold her attention for quite some time, and there are a variety of household objects which make very good toys for bathtime play. A colander and funnel each let water drain away in different ways; yogurt containers and margarine tubs float and are light to handle even when full of water, and you can pierce holes in them to make delightful sprinklers; plastic bottles and ice-cream

Water toys

Household objects can be adapted to add variety to a collection of toys designed for bathtime play.

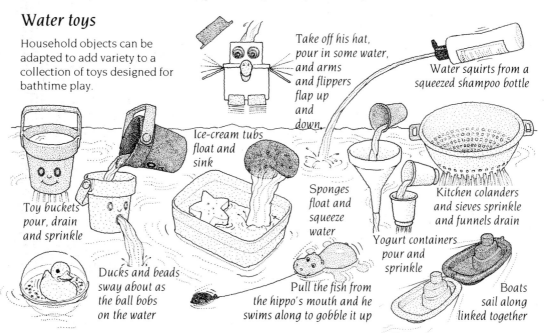

Take off his hat, pour in some water, and arms and flippers flap up and down.

Water squirts from a squeezed shampoo bottle

Ice-cream tubs float and sink

Toy buckets pour, drain and sprinkle

Sponges float and squeeze water

Kitchen colanders and sieves sprinkle and funnels drain

Yogurt containers pour and sprinkle

Ducks and beads sway about as the ball bobs on the water

Pull the fish from the hippo's mouth and he swims along to gobble it up

Boats sail along linked together

With armbands and your hand supporting him, your baby can feel quite secure and thoroughly enjoy the novel experience of floating on his back.

containers can also be adapted for emptying and sprinkling. Sponges can be cut into various shapes, and are easy for your baby to grasp and fun to squeeze out.

Although she cannot yet get the most out of all these interesting objects, she will enjoy it if you invent your own games. You can empty a yogurt container once, twice, three times into an ice-cream container and then pour all the water out into the bath with a loud 'SPLASH'. The skill as always is in the timing, keeping the 'SPLASH' until just the right moment so that she waits in excited anticipation for the final climax.

If you want to bathe a baby and toddler together in a shallow bath, you can sit the baby in a laundry basket, placed on a rubber bathmat, where she can play safely while you wash the toddler.

Learning to swim at home

Now is a good time to start to teach your baby to swim. You can do so in a bath filled with enough warm water for her to float in. She must be wearing either inflatable armbands or a life preserver to keep her afloat and, as you may find it difficult to get a life

preserver that is small enough to fit without slipping off, armbands are probably the safest solution until she is a few months older.

Once she is fully equipped, lower her gently into the bath, supporting her under her chest with your hand – she should be able to keep her head clear of the water for fairly long periods by this stage. Just let her enjoy splashing and get her used to the water on her face as you move her gently up and down. Once she's used to this position, you can try her on her back as well. Remember never to leave her alone in the bath, not even for a few seconds.

Playing with toys together . . . .

It is through her games with you that she becomes interested in the world of objects. Left to her own devices, she would show little interest in toys, but because she is interested in you, she becomes interested in the toy you are showing her. She watches the way you move a rattle and listens to the rhythms you tap out and the words that accompany your play.

The most rewarding games you can play are those in which you build on what she can do with your own words, sounds and actions. In this way you let her set the pace and encourage her to join in whenever she can. She loves games which repeat short sequences with their own sounds and words, each building up to a small climax. You can make a tower for her out of light plastic tubs and show her how to knock it down. If she's not yet ready to knock it down herself, just let her have the fun of watching your performance. I've seen babies wait in delighted suspense for the final collapse, greeting it with great excitement – waving arms, broad smiles and squeals of enjoyment.

Once she can sit alone on the floor, you can put a collection of toys and other interesting objects in a box and show her how to take them out. She'll get great enjoyment from the type of toy that is weighted at the bottom and impossible to knock over.

It goes without saying that many of the games you play together will be without any toys at all. All those physical games – tickling, cuddles and hugs, lifting her up and down and imitating her noises – continue to amuse her, and you'll find yourself expanding these games to match her new talents. As you play these simple games together, you may find yourself repeating words and phrases such as "all fall down" and "one ... two ... three ... and over she goes". Over the months she'll come to associate your words with actions and events as well as with objects – an important association to make for future language development.

You can also introduce her to toys that she'll soon be ready to play with alone. But don't expect them to keep her amused for

Totally engrossed in watching you build a tower, she can hardly wait for you to finish your turn before gleefully reaching out to knock it down.

Action toys

This collection of attractive and rewarding toys encourages your baby to use her hands in many different ways.

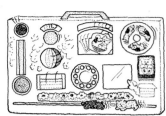

Activity center
Different manual skills – pushing, turning, rolling, dialing – produce a variety of sound and movement

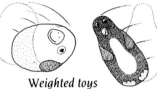

Water center
Pouring water and pushing buttons produce a flurry of activity as water wheels turn

Activity bear
Pulling a watch and twisting a bow tie are just two of the skills required to set this bear in motion

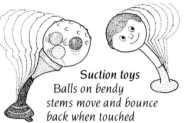

Suction toys
Balls on bendy stems move and bounce back when touched

Weighted toys
Wobbly animals bob up again when your baby knocks them down

more than a short period, as her concentration span is very short and there's so much around to distract her. There are various ingenious collections of toys that you can buy, all contained within the same frame, known as baby centers or activity centers. They are bright and colorful and encourage your baby to use her hands in different ways – pulling, pushing, dialing and so on. When she does so, she is rewarded by pictures changing, bells ringing and horns sounding. Although some of the activities which the center contains may still be too difficult for your baby, she'll soon be able to manage quite a few just from watching you. You can either put the center beside her on the floor or attach it to the side of her crib so she can play with it when she's alone.

Household objects

One thing you can be certain of is that your baby will get just as much fun out of playing with ordinary household objects that don't have to be specially bought. You may have noticed how she often shows more interest in the wrapping paper or packaging that a toy arrives in than in the toy itself (see page 78). This is not surprising as it has so many attractive qualities for her – it makes interesting rustling sounds, there's lots of it to grab, and even if she drops it she can easily find it again. The lightness of paper or cardboard means that she can hold great expanses of it in her hands, unlike other objects she is used to holding which usually have to be quite small. At present, she tends to use her playthings for waving, swiping and banging, and packaging is fun to play with in this way.

·UNDERSTANDING THE WORLD·

By now your baby has collected together quite a lot more information about the world around her, but acquiring it is not enough. She also needs to 'digest' it, to organize or file it away with other similar pieces of information so it relates to what she already knows.

In recent years developmental psychologists have devoted a great deal of time to researching the ways in which a baby's powers of thought and understanding develop and operate. Many of them believe that a baby organizes all the fresh information she receives as though through a sort of filing system [36]. Sometimes she finds that the system she has been using so far is unable to cope with a new experience so she has to adapt it in order to come to terms with the new material. For a baby, such an experience may be as simple as the sight of her father for the first time without his beard!

You may have noticed a look of momentary confusion when you end a familiar game with a slightly different twist. If she's used to you bouncing her up and down on your knee to the familiar words of "bumpety ... bumpety ... bumpety ... bump", and one day you change this familiar rhythm so that it ends with an "and over you go" as you tip her gently backwards, she may look surprised and even a little alarmed. But the next time you play the same game, she may be waiting in excited anticipation for the final twist.

When we think, we make use of abstract ideas, words and logic to organize all the information we receive, but a baby has none of these means at her command. Her knowledge of something is based on how it looks, tastes, sounds and feels, and she comes to know her own body in a similar way. For her, a rattle is its physical characteristics: the noise it makes; the feel of its weight in her hand; the way it tastes and smells, and the feeling she experiences in her hand, wrist and arm as she shakes it. Much of her understanding of people is also very physical, but through her own sociability and your responsiveness she is lead into the world of communication and social relationships.

Memory

Her memory at this stage is still limited to recognition of familiar faces and voices, and experiences she has come across before – she doesn't yet seem able to call something to mind when it is no longer physically present. Although she may become very excited each time you lower her into the bath, it's unlikely that she lies awake in her crib thinking about the nice time she had in the bath an hour ago. Similarly, she may cry if you leave her, because she was enjoying your company, but it is unlikely she'll spend time thinking about you when you're no longer present.

OPPOSITE *Half hiding a favorite toy (top left), catches her attention and she leans forward to pull it out (top right), holding it up triumphantly for you to see (below).*

BELOW *Puzzled and yet fascinated by the face he sees in the mirror, your baby is still too young to realize that it is an image of himself.*

From about six months onwards, she'll love to sit on your knee and look into a mirror, although it won't be until well into her first year that she makes the connection between what she sees in the mirror and herself. For the moment she is quite happy just watching the changing reflections as she moves. There are some specially designed baby mirrors on the market which are quite safe for her to play with, bite on and generally bang about. Some can be attached to her crib and she may find looking in the mirror totally absorbing, but only for short periods of time.

She'll start to enjoy simple games of hide-and-seek at about seven months. Let her watch you hide a toy under a piece of cloth with half of it showing, and then ask her to find it. Don't cover it completely, as she's then unlikely to attempt to remove the cloth – she hasn't yet come to realize that things continue to exist even when they are no longer visible.

· COMMUNICATING ·

Your baby's getting better and better at expressing how she feels. She squeals and wriggles with delight when she sees her food coming or when you give her one of her favorite toys to hold, and at about six months she may even show you how pleased she is to see you by holding out her arms for you to lift her up. When she's angry or disappointed or desperate for something, she lets you know by the expression on her face and the clamor she makes, reaching out towards the thing she wants. To a certain extent she's controlling her world through you – she can get you to remove something which is causing her discomfort, just as she can get you to retrieve a lost toy.

Old and new friends

There are bound to be many familiar figures in her life by this stage. Siblings, grandparents and babysitters have all had the chance to get to know her and, because they are sensitive to her, she is always glad of their familiar, comforting presence. She still takes to strangers fairly easily and will let them comfort and amuse her if you leave her alone with them for a short while, although it may take a little time for them to be able to recognize and respond to all her little signals. If you have friends and relations who live at quite a distance who want to come and meet her for the first time, now is a good time to invite them. Later on, she will become much more cautious with people she doesn't know, and in some cases even wary of them – you may have noticed how much easier it is to get a smile from a baby of this age than it is from one who is slightly older.

Everyone she encounters will have their particular style of playing and communicating with her. Research has shown that in our society fathers play in a more boisterous, physical way with their babies than mothers, who mostly have a quieter style and are more likely to introduce toys into their play [37]. Whether this is because women are expected to behave differently from men or whether it is because of innate differences is open to question. Some research suggests that a father does not behave differently just because he sees less of the baby and is therefore readier for more noisy games; in fact the results show that even those fathers who have the principal role in looking after their babies still play with them in a more boisterous fashion [38].

Other babies

Babies are interested in and react to other babies right from birth. An example of this is the way in which newborn babies cry when they hear another baby crying [39]. During the first two months of life, babies just gaze at each other as objects of mutual interest, but by six months their enjoyment in each other's company really

Babies are often affectionate and direct with one another — reaching out to touch and feel, gazing into each other's eyes and smiling warmly.

starts to show. If you haven't already done so, now is a good time to visit a mother and baby group, where your baby will have the chance to meet other babies of a similar age.

As long as you choose a time when your baby is neither tired nor upset, she will smile delightedly on being introduced to another baby and try to reach out to make contact. Take care in case they should hurt one another in their enthusiasm – you may well have to restrain their small hands from poking eyes or pulling hair as they investigate each other thoroughly.

Psychologists have suggested that such meetings are particularly interesting and stimulating for a baby of this age because the actions and sounds of another baby are precisely those she's tuned into. At the same time, the other baby is not making the sort of controlled efforts that an adult makes when trying to communicate, and so her behavior comes across as that much more varied and unexpected, and yet not threatening.

Making sounds . . . .

At about four months, she starts to make a rather pretty gentle sound, a sort of cooing "agoo" and she loves you to join in with her, saying the sound back to her. She may even repeat the sound after you once she is able to produce it spontaneously. She also develops a more boisterous selection of sounds, amusing herself by spluttering and blowing raspberries, and will soon be able to imitate new sounds that you make to her.

Earlier on you may have noticed her making small movements with her lips and tongue – pushing her tongue out between her gums or teeth, bringing her lips together and then releasing them as she breathes out a small bubble of saliva. Some developmental psychologists believe that these early movements, which co-ordinate breathing with tongue and lip articulation, are a baby's first attempts at speech.

At around seven months, she starts to make sounds which are more and more like those found in adult speech – producing consonants like 'b' using her lips and 'd' using her tongue. Syllables like 'ba' and 'da' also make an appearance about now.

Rhymes and songs

One of the most enjoyable aspects of bringing up a baby is that you can join in all sorts of activities that might not occur to you in other situations – singing to another person is just one of them. She'll listen intently when you sing songs and lullabies to her, and is bound to enjoy old favorites like Twinkle Twinkle Little Star and Ba Ba Black Sheep.

At around six months, you can introduce her to finger games when she's sitting on your knee. Try this one, counting on her fingers as you go:

One two three four five,
Once I caught a fish alive,
Six seven eight nine ten,
Then I let it go again.
Why did you let it go?
Because it bit my finger so.
Which finger did it bite?
This little finger on the right (taking her little finger and joggling it up and down).

As you play with her, other old favorites may come to mind. "This little piggy went to market" and "Round and round the garden" are both rhymes which she will enjoy:

This little piggy went to market (taking her big toe),
This little piggy stayed at home (taking her second toe),
This little piggy had roast beef (taking her third toe),
And this little piggy had none (taking her fourth toe),
And this little piggy went wee, wee, wee,
All the way home (taking her little toe, then running your fingers up her leg and body to hide them at the top).

Round and round the garden (circling one finger round her palm),
Like a Teddy bear,
One step (walking one finger one step up her arm),
Two step (taking another step with the second finger),
And tickly under there (tickling under her arm).

These rhymes will stand endless repetition and you will find that the more often you do them, the more your baby will enjoy them. She loves watching your fingers and listening to your voice, connecting the two and waiting all the time for the final surprise. You can play either of these games with her fingers or her toes.

Sharing her interests . . . .

A baby will learn most from the things that interest her, and research has shown that mothers react accordingly — they are sensitive to any sight or sound that attracts their baby's attention and will talk to her about it [40]. What is important for the baby is that the person who is close to her — whether mother, father or other caregiver — shares her experience and names it for her. You may have noticed her excitement, her wide open eyes and outstretched arms, when you bring her her favorite food and talk to her about it saying: "You like that, don't you? ... M'm it's good, isn't it?" In this way you are tuning into her interest, sharing her focus and turning her individual experience into a joint experience, something both of you can share and enjoy together.

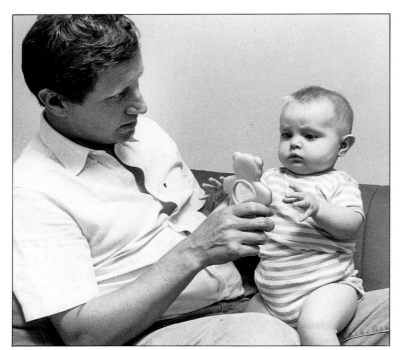

If you talk to her about the toy she is investigating (top), she may lift her eyes to meet yours as though trying to understand what you have to say (bottom).

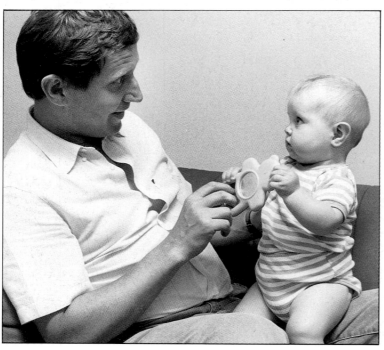

Sharing her interest is quite different from pointing things out to her and then naming them. In fact you will probably have noticed by now that it's difficult to get her to pay attention to something 'out there' if she hasn't already noticed it herself. This is partly because she cannot yet follow the direction of your finger when you point something out. However, you can get her to notice objects at close range if you play with them and move them in a way that catches her attention.

Outings

Now that your baby can sit up, outings in the stroller or in the car provide her with many new sights and sounds, and shopping trips to the park and visits to friends all provide new experiences and different things for you to talk to her about. When you take her to the park, let her get out of her stroller and support her standing up where she can see a duck or a squirrel almost on a level with herself. In the supermarket, you can sit her in one of the specially designed seats and let her look at the shelves of colorful goods, and talk to her about them as you shop. On occasions like these, you will find yourself seeing the world through her eyes as she looks around, attracted perhaps by the movement of a bird or animal or the bright colors of boxes and cans stacked up in the supermarket.

Outings to the local supermarket may be routine for you, but your baby may find them thrilling – riding along in a cart gives him a wonderful view of everything going on around him.

ON THE MOVE
· · · · · · · · · · · ·
8–12 MONTHS

Introduction . . . .

If you watch your baby during the last months of his first year, you'll see a young explorer, increasingly on the move: rolling on the carpet, scuttling away from you on all fours when you try to catch him, cruising around the room using the furniture for support, and ultimately, taking his first unaided steps.

In contrast to this spirit of adventure are his sudden need for the security of familiar people and places and his growing wariness of strangers. He starts to cling to you, worrying about losing sight of you and wanting to follow you wherever you go. You may find this sudden change in his behavior difficult to cope with, but it will help if you can see it for what it is – a clear indication of his growing ability to understand and remember. He's beginning to realize the possible implications of your leaving him, so you'll need to prepare him for a parting, making sure he has had time to get to know and feel at ease with the adult you leave him with.

· ACQUIRING PHYSICAL SKILLS ·

He's coming to the age when he can choose for himself whether he lies down, sits or stands up, and he's really starting to move. Combining this new-found mobility with his rapidly developing manual dexterity, he's now able to get hold of and thoroughly investigate many of the objects which attract his attention.

Rolling

At about six months he starts to roll from front to back, but doesn't really start to get about under his own steam until sometime around seven or eight months, when he first rolls over from back to front. This new achievement involves quite a lot of effort on his part, but, once mastered, he's then able to roll in a full circle – from front to back and then over again from back to front. By repeating these movements, he can roll little by little across the floor. Some babies take to rolling as a principal means of getting around and are soon able to cover quite a lot of ground in this way.

Creeping and crawling

He first starts to creep at about nine months. He's not yet able to lift his tummy off the ground but he can still manage to pull himself along the floor, although to begin with he'll probably go backwards! He may impress you by adopting a swimming technique, pushing off with his toes in such a way that he is able to move along the floor quite quickly. Soon after he begins to creep, he'll start to crawl properly, lifting his tummy off the floor, and eventually building up quite a speed, racing about on all fours.

Some babies never go through the crawling stage at all, but move about extraordinarily efficiently just by sitting up and shuffling forwards on their bottoms. They stretch out a leg (or both legs in some cases) and pull their body forward by flexing at the knee.

Whether a crawler or shuffler, every room will become a place for adventure and physical exploration. He'll examine the table from underneath, crawl behind the sofa, chase toys into corners and under cupboards, and investigate thoroughly behind the curtain and under the chair. In these early days, he may frequently get stuck and cry out for you to rescue him, but he'll soon become an adept adventurer, covering the floor rapidly, already familiar with intricate features of his territory – the table and chair legs, the castors under the television table or the base and stem of a floor lamp. With his knees and hands, he'll get to know the textures of different floor coverings – smooth cool plastic, soft carpet and woolly rugs.

Crawling into large cardboard boxes is something he'll enjoy at this age. You can push out the end of a box so he can crawl right through it, or even better, line up a collection of large boxes to form a tunnel. He'll soon be able to play follow-the-leader, crawling after you through the tunnel, out, round and back again.

Balls and rolling toys

Brightly colored balls and rolling toys are fascinating and fun for him to chase after, as are toy animals on wheels, and cars and trucks of various sizes. Lots of household objects, such as empty plastic bottles, cartons and containers, are round and roll, not as smoothly as a ball perhaps, but he'll still enjoy chasing after them. Some of the time he'll play spontaneously in this way, but he'll always enjoy it more when you play together – you rolling the ball for him to fetch or racing against him as he chases after it.

Standing up

He's coming closer and closer to taking his first unsupported steps, but, as with crawling, he will reach walking in stages. By nine

Rolling toys

As soon as your baby starts to crawl, you can give him rolling toys to chase after – brightly colored ones and those that make a noise as they move.

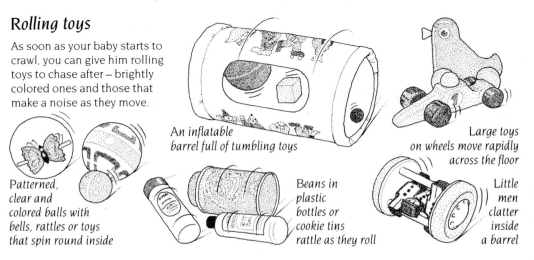

Patterned, clear and colored balls with bells, rattles or toys that spin round inside

An inflatable barrel full of tumbling toys

Beans in plastic bottles or cookie tins rattle as they roll

Large toys on wheels move rapidly across the floor

Little men clatter inside a barrel

From lying to walking

Creeping
Soon after, he starts to creep, keeping his tummy close to the ground and propelling himself along by pushing off with his feet and pulling with his arms.

Rolling
He really starts to move about by himself when he first learns to roll · *from back to front and so is able to complete a full circle.*

months he may well pull himself up to standing, using furniture or the bars of his crib, and shortly after this he will be able to walk supporting himself and keeping his balance by holding on to convenient pieces of furniture – chair seats and arms and the edges of low tables. He cruises along in this way with shuffling sideways steps, moving one foot to the side and then bringing the other foot up to meet it. If you hold both his hands for the sake of balance, he can step forward towards you. A little later, one hand will do.

Walking unaided

Once he can stand alone, you can look forward to the day when he takes his first unaided steps. Most babies walk at some time between ten and fourteen months, although some may do so as early as nine months and others not until eighteen months. Walking requires great feats of balance and co-ordination, and you'll see from the expression on your baby's face what an adventure it is for him to take the risk of stepping out. It is a very rewarding experience for you when you hold out your hands to him to take his first steps towards you; it's also a great achievement for him to be able to get around on just two feet, with his hands left free for other activities.

Push-along toys

The heavier type of push-along toy will come in useful at this stage, as he can lean on it for support as he walks along and it's unlikely to run away from him. When you buy a baby walker, make sure it is well-designed so it does not topple backwards when he leans on it. To begin with, even a baby walker filled with blocks will need extra weighting down if he is to use it for pulling himself up to standing. Later on, he will be able to manage toy animals on wheels, and balls which can be pushed along on the end of a stick.

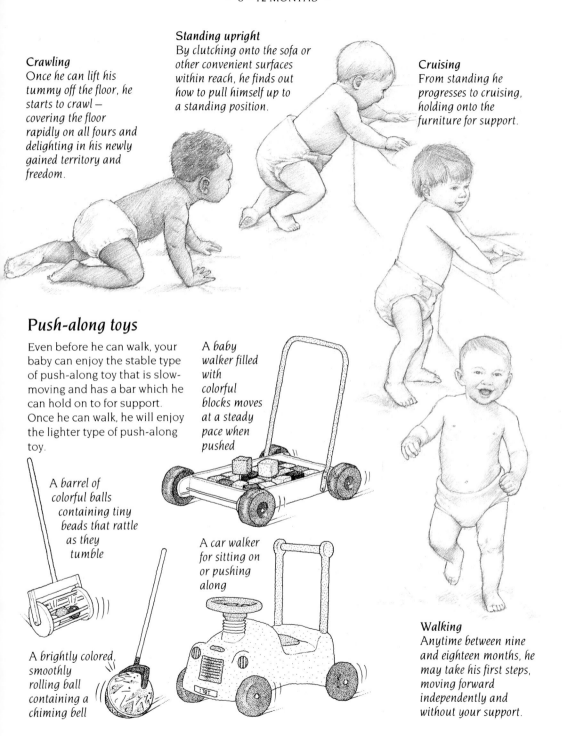

Crawling
Once he can lift his tummy off the floor, he starts to crawl — covering the floor rapidly on all fours and delighting in his newly gained territory and freedom.

Standing upright
By clutching onto the sofa or other convenient surfaces within reach, he finds out how to pull himself up to a standing position.

Cruising
From standing he progresses to cruising, holding onto the furniture for support.

Push-along toys

Even before he can walk, your baby can enjoy the stable type of push-along toy that is slow-moving and has a bar which he can hold on to for support. Once he can walk, he will enjoy the lighter type of push-along toy.

A baby walker filled with colorful blocks moves at a steady pace when pushed

A barrel of colorful balls containing tiny beads that rattle as they tumble

A car walker for sitting on or pushing along

A brightly colored, smoothly rolling ball containing a chiming bell

Walking
Anytime between nine and eighteen months, he may take his first steps, moving forward independently and without your support.

Reaching

He has developed a variety of ways for getting hold of things that he wants. He can reach out for something either by leaning forward from a sitting position or by simply rolling over towards it. As he becomes increasingly mobile, he will crawl, and finally walk, to the object or person attracting his attention.

If an object attracts his attention, he'll do everything he can to get hold of it, and once he has it, he will investigate it very thoroughly. Now is the time when he starts to open cupboards and remove the contents. You'll probably find it easiest if you can come to a compromise and allow him access to one or two kitchen cupboards in which you keep unbreakable objects such as plastic containers, while keeping the others locked or securely fastened. The surest way to keep him out of harm's way is to remove anything that he can damage or that could hurt him, by locking it away or putting it safely out of his reach. He can't yet tell the difference between his toys and other valuable, possibly fragile, household belongings, so once again it's probably best to keep these out of his way. If he does try to grab hold of a valued ornament or plant, you may be able to distract him as you take it from him, by offering him an interesting toy or game.

Handling

As his movements become more skilled and co-ordinated, he stops grasping things in the palm of his hand and starts to hold them more carefully between fingers and thumb. At nine months, he uses a pincer-like grip to pick up really quite small objects, such as a crumb of bread or a raisin, but in order to do so successfully he must have a hard surface on which to rest his hand.

During this period, he also starts to use his forefinger to poke into holes and other objects, but it will be a while yet before he uses it to point things out to other people. Depending on his mood at the time, he may poke his finger into his food or grab a fistful of it – there's no telling what line his investigations will take, so be prepared for mealtimes to be messy.

Now that he can handle two objects at once, new opportunities for play are opening up. For example, blocks become fun for banging together; a plastic cup makes an interesting noise when it is scraped up and down on a tabletop and a saucepan makes an exciting noise when it's banged with a wooden spoon.

Letting go

He can't release his grip intentionally until he reaches about nine or ten months old. This means that until then he cannot give you an object. He may offer you something, but you will have to help him release his grip before you can take it out of his hand.

Once he can release his hold on things, at about twelve months, he'll enjoy playing games of give and take, passing toys backwards and forwards between you. He may even pass you his food – a cracker or a piece of banana – for you to have a taste!

Allowing your baby access to one of your kitchen cupboards can provide him with an endless source of amusement and fun.

Making music with wooden spoons and metal pans can become a favorite occupation, although from time to time even he may find the noise a bit too much to bear!

Toys for taking apart

To start with, he drops things accidentally, but by the time he's a year old he's actually got the knack of throwing things down from his high chair or out of his crib. It's a game he'll particularly enjoy, especially if you respond by handing the toy back to him – as always he prefers games which you can play together. You may become tired and irritated by this particular game the more he plays it, but take comfort in the knowledge that it's only likely to last until he's about fifteen months old.

He loves to take things apart at this age, but it will be a while yet before he can put them back together again. Nesting toys – sets of cubes or cylinders which fit snugly into one another according to size – and boats of peg people can all be easily taken apart, but he'll need you there to put them back together again.

Around about the end of his first year, he'll start to enjoy simple lift-out puzzles of the type which have loose pieces with knobs attached for him to grasp hold of. You'll have just enough time to put the pieces back in place for him before he starts to take them out again. Mail boxes and similar toys will also begin to interest him around the end of his first year. You can make your own out of large plastic ice-cream boxes with different size holes cut into the lid and an assortment of objects to "mail".

Other popular toys include snaplock beads which he will just wave around to begin with. Eventually, he will learn to pull them apart, but only much later will he learn how to put them back together again. Lightweight foam or plastic blocks can be adapted for a variety of activities. He may even try to make a tower with them if he's watched you build one, but it's unlikely that he'll succeed in doing so just yet.

Toys to pull apart

He now enjoys toys he can pull apart or take to pieces and loves to involve you in his games, waiting for you to put them back together again. By watching you, he will learn how to put them back together.

Small knobs make it easy to lift out large puzzle pieces

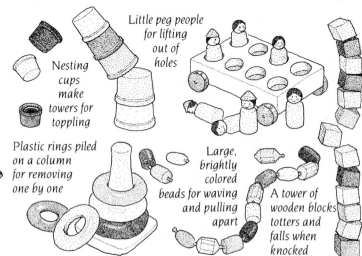

Little peg people for lifting out of holes

Nesting cups make towers for toppling

Plastic rings piled on a column for removing one by one

Large, brightly colored beads for waving and pulling apart

A tower of wooden blocks totters and falls when knocked

SAFETY IN THE HOME

He no longer stays where you put him so it's important to be aware of and protect against any possible hazards in the rooms where he spends his time. If you need to leave him alone for a few minutes, place him somewhere he can come to no harm. Remember that even if you have made the room totally safe, he may still be able to roll over to the door and be hurt by someone opening it from the other side, so it's best to leave him harnessed into his stroller or infant seat, or safe in a crib or playpen, while you are out of the room. At this age, a playpen with a floor is safer than one without, as once he can stand he will be able to move a floorless playpen across the room by pushing it in front of him.

- Make sure there are no trailing cords or tablecloths that he can pull on, bringing things tumbling down on top of him

- Keep bottles containing bleach, strong cleaners, disinfectant or any other harmful substances out of reach on a high shelf or in an inaccessible cupboard. Remember that your baby may soon be able to open low unlocked cupboards

- Keep bottles of medicine and pills in a locked medicine chest

- Keep sharp or pointed instruments, electrical tools and appliances in a safe place out of your baby's reach

- Make sure that all heating appliances and fires have childproof guards – even a hot radiator can burn delicate skin

- Use a stove guard around the top of the stove to prevent him from pulling saucepans down on top of him, or make sure that the handles of the saucepans are facing inwards

- Until he reaches about eleven or twelve months, he still likes to explore everything with his mouth as well as with his hands and eyes, so make sure there are no swallowable objects like pins, pills or buttons lying around that he can pick up and pop into his mouth. Some houseplants are poisonous, so make sure that any you possess are placed well out of his reach

---

Outdoor play . . . .

At this age, your baby is increasingly interested in the outside world and will show his excitement when you get his stroller out ready to take him outside. Walks, outings to the shops and visits to friends all take on a new dimension now that he's so much more aware of his surroundings and ready to learn from you. There's so much to interest and amuse him, and many new things to do.

The swimming pool   If your baby has come to enjoy the experience of floating and playing with you in the bath, then now may be a good time to take him to the swimming pool for the first time. Many of the newer pools have a separate baby or 'training' pool in which the water is kept at a slightly higher temperature than in the main pool. Some pools have special sessions for babies and toddlers, so they can

An ice-cream container with holes cut out of the lid makes an ideal mail box for a year-old baby.

get used to water gently without being splashed or frightened by the boisterous play of older children. If your pool doesn't have this facility, try to choose a fairly quiet time of the day, at least for your first few visits. You may even be lucky enough to have the option of attending baby swimming classes where you can help your baby develop his skills with the benefit of expert advice and in the company of other adults and babies.

Teachers vary in the methods they adopt for teaching babies to swim, so if you do decide to attend classes, it's probably a good idea to go along beforehand to watch a class in progress and to see whether you like the teacher's general approach. Whether you go to lessons or not, there is much you can do yourself to make your baby's introduction to the swimming pool a happy and pleasant experience that he will be eager to repeat. At this stage the most important thing is that he should enjoy himself and learn to feel totally confident in water.

First visit

You can start your first session in the pool by carrying him into the shallow end and walking about in the water without even getting him wet. If your pool has wide shallow steps covered with a few inches of water, the ideal next stage is to allow him to sit and pat or splash the water or play with a small water toy so that he has the chance to get used to the environment with its new sounds and smell of chlorine.

Five or ten minutes may be enough for his first visit but if you think he is ready to go on, you might like to try the next stage of gradually immersing him up to his shoulders while you hold him securely under his arms. Bob him up and down for a while and let him get used to the feel of water as it splashes on his face.

He may be a bit apprehensive at first, so don't be surprised if he cries. Just keep your visits short, take each new stage very gently and keep smiling and talking to him, showing him that you're enjoying yourself and that it's all meant to be fun. If you let him progress at his own pace, he will move on more happily and confidently to the next stage.

Subsequent visits

On your next visit you will probably be able to carry him straight into the water. Then, with your hands supporting him securely under the arms as he faces you, you can crouch down so your head

Enjoying the pool
*Once your baby is used
to water and feels
confident enough to
paddle along without
your help, armbands
and a close-fitting life
preserver will give him
the support he needs. He
can now bob about
independently with you
close at hand.*

*Once he is used to the
pool, he'll love you to
pull him along at
different speeds,
watching your smiling
face all the while.*

is on a level with his just above the water, and pull him gently
through the water towards you. Gradually, as the sessions progress,
you can encourage him to use his arms and legs in a 'doggy paddle'
and get him used to water being splashed over his face as he kicks
and paddles.

You can follow this by letting him get used to being on his back
and, eventually, having his ears under water. Hold him so that his
head is against your chest, his body between your arms and your
hands supporting his thighs. From this position you can gradually
move away from him, sliding your hands up to support him under
his arms. Talk and toys are useful to distract him when he is doing
something new, so try giving him a rattle to play with while you are
introducing him to being on his back. Once he is happy in this
position, you can walk backwards, supporting him under his
shoulders and drawing him through the water.

Once your baby starts to have less need of your support, you can
get him used to armbands and/or a life preserver, making sure the
life preserver fits properly so there is no risk of him slipping
through. With these to keep him afloat, he can kick his legs freely
and learn to move through the water independently. Learning to
use his legs is an important first step in learning to swim, although
he will still be in a fairly upright position at this stage.

In swimming classes babies soon learn to paddle about
supported by a life preserver. Again, toys are used, but this time to
attract them rather than distract them, so that they move through
the water towards them. At this age they do not go very far and
should always have an adult at their side, ready to lift them out of
the water when they are tired or in need of a rest.

Points to remember
• Your baby should have had at least two sets of immunizations
before you take him to a public pool for the first time. In any case,
check with your doctor beforehand if you are worried about your
baby's health, or in any way uncertain as to whether or not you
should take him to the pool

- Don't take him to the pool if he has a cold or any other infection
- The temperature of the water in the pool should be no lower than 27°C (80°F) and the changing area should also be warm
- It's important your baby does not get cold, so avoid leaving him without any clothes on for any length of time
- Dress him in a close-fitting pair of pants. There's no need for him to wear a diaper – it will only become waterlogged and drag him down – and pants are an adequate protection in the unlikely event that he soils himself
- If he feels the cold or dislikes being without his clothes, then it may help if you leave a sleeveless undershirt on him when he goes into the water, at least until he feels more relaxed
- Take a towel with you to the poolside, so you can wrap him up and start to dry him immediately when you take him out of the water

Water play outdoors

Children of different ages can play happily together in a wading pool – each enjoying his own particular toy, and occasionally stopping to watch the others play.

In summer you can set up an inflatable wading pool out of doors, which will provide wonderful opportunities for play on warm summer days. You need only fill the pool with about 8 inches of water but make sure it is comfortably warm by topping it off with hot water. Give your baby his favorite bathtime toys to play with, and anything else that floats and is fun to splash or tip up when it's full of water. He still finds it difficult to empty things neatly but he loves to dash after floating toys, and to splash about in the water with you.

· UNDERSTANDING THE WORLD ·

At the same time as his ability to reach and handle things is developing, his understanding of the world around him is coming closer to an adult's conception of reality and less confined to the immediate information he receives through his senses. Research has shown that at about this age a baby starts to realize that people, things and events have a separate existence from himself and are not limited to the immediate present [41].

You will notice many signs of this new awareness – when he drops a toy, for instance, he leans over the stroller or crib to see where it has gone. He now knows that it has not ceased to exist just because it has rolled out of sight, and he may even cry for you to retrieve it. If you attach the toy to a piece of string, he may learn to pull it back himself. He starts to follow things and people with his eyes as they go out of sight, and waits for them to reappear again – watching the door, for example, after someone leaves. He enjoys games of peek-a-boo when you peep out at him from behind a piece of cloth or a pillow or even just from behind your closed hands, either partially covering your face or hiding it completely. You can now play more advanced games of hide and seek – hiding something completely under a cloth or in a box while he watches you, and then asking him to find it again. He may recover it instantly and wave it about excitedly.

His memory, for so long limited to recognition of things and people met before, is now developing in major ways. He's beginning to recall earlier experiences and can now bring you to mind when you are no longer present. But to begin with he will only be able to store things in his memory for very short periods of time [42].

Planning ahead

In order to plan his actions, he needs to know that objects have permanence and to remember how events have worked out in the past. He now has these abilities, even though they are still very rudimentary, and is far from the stage when his actions were a fairly automatic response.

When he was newborn, he already had the ability to learn, probably through association and recognition, that he could make things happen. Remember the baby who learned to turn his head when a bell sounded, in order to be rewarded by sweet water (see page 38). He still uses association and recognition in this way, but new mental processes that develop about this time make him much more deliberate in his actions, and also enable him to make surer predictions about the consequences of his interactions with other people and his environment.

Hiding your face behind a pillow may produce a response of mild suspense (*top*). Take the pillow away and the suspense instantly gives way to relief and delighted laughter (*bottom*).

• COMMUNICATING •

The ways in which he joins in your activities and rituals together show that he is developing further towards being a communicating person. He shows that he understands some of the meanings that your words and actions contain, and that he remembers sequences of action and patterns in the way people behave. His own feelings about people and about what is happening are more clearly expressed and so easier to understand. For example, the sound of mother or father or an older brother or sister returning home – a key turning in the lock or a footstep on the stair – produces hushed expectancy and then smiles and arms outstretched in recognition.

It is not only events that he responds to. He's also sensitive to your facial expression and can tell when you're pleased or cross about something. Words are also starting to carry meaning for him. By eight months, he may have some understanding of the word "no". You can even make him aware that you don't like what he is trying to do by saying "no", but don't expect him to respond by stopping what he is doing. He also comes, around this age, to recognize and respond to his own name.

Letting you know how he feels

Crying and smiling are still powerful signals which have an affect on those around him, but he's developing a wider repertoire now, and is becoming, by the week, increasingly clever at finding ways of attracting your attention and letting you know what he wants. He pulls at your trouser leg or skirt to get you to notice him and shakes his head vigorously if he doesn't want something. If he sees you coming to remove something he's particularly enjoying, he shakes his head so you have no doubt of his meaning, and scuttles off in the opposite direction.

Most days he'll show his pleasure at being with you by co-operating in your daily rituals – holding out his arm to go into a sleeve or his foot to go into a sock or shoe. At other times, he'll make it very clear that he's feeling unco-operative by making his body rigid as you try to dress him, or by pushing away a spoon or screwing up his face, frustrating your attempts to feed him.

Unfamiliar adults

Most babies now start to show wariness and caution on meeting unfamiliar adults. Psychologists often attribute this sudden change in their behavior to their developing ability to remember [43]. Now that they can bring to mind people with whom they are familiar, they start to be shy and wary when introduced to people they do not know very well.

However, if you give them the chance to get to know a stranger from the safety of your lap, their initial wariness will soon turn to smiles and friendly curiosity.

Other babies

If you give your baby the opportunity to mix with other babies and toddlers, he will learn from an early age how to get along with others and will make new friends with greater ease [44]. Babies delight in each other's company and, while they may be wary of unfamiliar adults, observations have shown that they are quite happy and unperturbed when introduced to unfamiliar babies [45]. Although mothers were present throughout these observations, the babies spent more time playing and interacting with their new friends than they did with their own mothers.

The more frequently babies meet and come to know other babies, the more they interact together and the more pleasure they find in each other's company. They eagerly approach one another and follow each other about, playing games like peek-a-boo together and, from about one year old, they may start to imitate the sounds that the other one makes.

The extent to which you participate in the meetings between your baby and other babies will affect how they get on together. For example, if you give them a toy to play with between them, this encourages them to interact together as they are both concentrating on the same object. At the same time, they are learning about each other and getting to know each other, and one important discovery they are bound to make is that they can have conflicting interests. Such conflicts will increase in the second year and may need some help from you to sort them out. However, they should not be seen as entirely negative experiences as it's important for your baby to learn how to face conflict and how to defend himself, as well as how to avoid confrontations by co-operating and learning to share his playthings with his playmates.

An interesting Danish research project, set in a daycare center, encouraged the staff to make a special effort to help babies become interested in each other and to encourage them to act in a co-operative way [46]. At mealtimes, the staff talked to the babies about each other, and at other times, they tried to engage them in activities together, giving them one ball to play with between two and encouraging games of give and take. The findings of the research showed that babies – even the very youngest – were much more responsive to one another than they had been before the staff had started to work in this manner.

Brothers and sisters

Your baby may have an older brother or sister who is his closest friend. Such a relationship can be very loving and rich in new experiences, but it will also have its stormy moments. Mixed feelings are often apparent – a toddler who is hugging and kissing his new baby brother or sister may pause from time to time, turn to his mother and ask in a hopeful tone of voice, "When is the baby going back to the hospital?"

A baby of this age will often miss his brother or sister when they are not present and may turn to them for love and comfort in distressing situations, even though they may have shown real hostility towards him at other times. The elder child may find the baby irritating if he interferes with a game and may react by pushing him roughly aside, but with time and your help the baby and toddler will learn to get on with each other. The older child will appreciate the novelty of having a responsible adult role to play – looking after the baby and taking the lead in play; while for the baby, part of the attraction will come from the fact that his brother or sister is so like himself. Older brothers or sisters will also have ideas for games – some quite advanced – which the baby can play as well. Such games need to be supervised, especially if the older child is still a toddler, as they can get quite rough and your baby is still too young to protect himself.

Signs, symbols and sounds . . . .

Your baby will acquire an understanding of gestures and the signs and symbols they contain before he starts to use spoken language. By about ten months he will start to imitate you, using the various gestures that he has learned from you. He plays peek-a-boo hiding his own face, claps his hands and joins in games of pat-a-cake. He may start to use objects in the ways in which you use them – attempting to brush his own hair, for example, or feeding you with his spoon. He also uses social gestures that he has learned from you. He waves 'bye-bye' and may pretend to blow a kiss, or at any rate he puts his hand to his mouth, even if he can't make the right kissing noise yet. By using these gestures at the right time, he shows you that he is coming to understand their meaning. If you imitate his sounds and actions back to him, he then has some feedback about what he is doing.

As well as using signs and symbols, he is also making rapid progress towards starting to talk. His babbles develop into repetitions of syllables – ba-ba, da-da-da-da – and he practices them endlessly, both for the pleasure of making the sounds and for the way they feel in his mouth. In this way he learns that, just as he can control his hands, so he can control his voice and the sounds he makes.

To start with, babies make similar sounds, whatever language is spoken around them, and they make them in the same sequence. But once a baby has gone through this basic sequence – which he will have by the time he is about one year old – he starts producing the sounds and intonation patterns of the language spoken around him, ignoring other possibilities. Using the sounds of this language, he spends a lot of time pretending to talk, having conversations with himself and with anyone else who is willing to join in. He can sound very convincing, in fact so much so that you may find yourself trying hard to understand what he is saying.

First words . . . .

Your baby may say his first word at any time after about 10 months, although there is quite a wide variation in the age at which babies do start to speak. It can be an exciting moment – hearing your baby speak for the first time – as not only does it give you further evidence of his developing powers of communication, it also means that his part in your conversations together takes on more importance as he starts to contribute more and more.

You'll notice that he understands some of the words you use before he starts to speak for himself. For example, he may respond to you when you say "Where's the car?" by looking towards the car, although he doesn't yet use the word 'car' himself. This ability to understand words and expressions before he uses them himself is something which will remain with him throughout childhood and probably throughout his life.

He is now able to store things in his memory for increasing lengths of time and so starts to use words to refer to things in their absence. "Da-da?" he inquires, using a rising, questioning tone when he hears a familiar step approaching. He makes his first words do a great deal of work and packs them with meaning. "Na-na! Na-na!" he shouts, making it quite clear that he wants his orange juice. At this stage, he may have his own words for things and may use one word to cover a variety of objects – "Ga-ga" may stand for cat, dog or hen, just because they all have similarities in his eyes. Adults who are familiar with him will be quick to grasp his meaning and may sometimes repeat the word back to him. There's no need to worry about using baby talk occasionally, as at least it lets him know he's making sense, and it also encourages him to keep experimenting with different words.

An important feature of language in general is that the meaning of a word depends to a large extent on the context in which it is used. For example, when your child says "door", you will know whether he means "open the door!" or "that's a door!" or "Mommy went out of the door", because you are aware of the circumstances in which the word is used. This compression of meanings into one word is typical of a baby's early attempts at language.

How babies acquire language

There is no simple and clear explanation of how a baby acquires language, but it is remarkable how quickly he does so. By the time he is 18 months old, he will be able to use some 50 words, to understand a good deal more and even start to put two words into short sentences.

While your baby may have an innate capacity for language, what is important is that he has been involved in conversations and games with you and others from the time he was only a few hours old. From these experiences, he has learned much about the process of communication. He has played turn-taking games and been involved in turn-taking talk – the basis of human conversation – and you have spoken to him in a variety of ways, engaging his attention by slowing your voice down, raising the pitch of your voice, repeating words and phrases and asking questions. In fact, you have generally behaved in such a way as to make language interesting for him.

Most important of all, the people with whom he has spent his waking hours have involved him in conversations about his immediate environment and its happenings. They have provided a commentary on the things he has seen and heard and on his feelings about them. They have given spoken labels to so many of the things that have caught his attention. It is these experiences more than anything else which underlie his early acquisition of language.

Familiar patterns and rituals . . . .

His developing understanding and memory and his increased ability to communicate mean that your baby appreciates the daily games and rituals you have built up together and recognizes them as they fit into his day, giving him a sense that life is orderly and secure. Getting up in the morning, mealtimes and bathtime are all part of the daily round. For some babies, saying goodbye to father or mother when they set off for work is an important feature of the day, as is greeting babysitters, other caregivers and perhaps other babies. Reunions at the end of the day also become something to look forward to.

If you are a working parent, you may want to spend a few quiet minutes with your baby when you first get home from work – adjusting to his rhythm. There are nearly always chores to be done, a meal to be prepared and eaten, but this too forms the pattern of his day. On a warm summer's evening, you may like to take him out for a short walk in the park or garden, or perhaps to visit friends who live nearby. If he's still full of energy by the end of the day, just before bathtime is a good time for rough and tumble games – rolling on the floor with him, or lifting him up into the air and swinging him down.

Music and rhythm

Songs can become a regular part of the evening routine. Your baby will enjoy rhythm and music, whether it is your own voice singing to him or music on the television or radio. He will join in dancing with you if you hold his hands, and will bob up and down

If you play your own musical instrument or sing, you can alter the tune, its timing and volume to suit your baby. To begin with, he'll listen intently but soon he may prefer to join in and sing along with you.

to the music. Sometimes he may even do so alone, holding on to furniture for support.

Research has shown that babies appreciate music and are already able to show their preference for one type of music over another. A study of babies' musical tastes was carried out by two psychologists who outfitted a cassette recorder in such a way that the babies could turn on the recorder themselves and choose which music to play to themselves in their cribs [47]. The babies often turned on the recorder and soon had their own favorite pieces of light music which they would play at frequent intervals. The study was carried out over a longish period and interestingly the babies' tastes soon moved away from light music to more classical pieces.

Favorite songs

Different cultures have different games and songs, and you may remember some from your own childhood. Riding games were a particular favorite with my own children, and they loved being jogged up and down on my knee to the rhythm of familiar nursery rhymes.

Once your baby sits securely on your knee, you can give him your

hands to hold for reins and bounce him up and down. Here are two songs which my own children enjoyed.

> To market, to market,
> To buy a fat pig,
> Home again, home again,
> Jiggety – jig.

> To market, to market,
> To buy a fat hog,
> Home again, home again,
> Jiggety – jog.

Suit the movements to the rhythm of the words in the song below and keep the final climax to the last line when you lower your baby down to the ground.

> This is the way the ladies ride – trit-trot, trit-trot, trit-trot
> This is the way the farmers ride – gallop, gallop, gallop
> This is the way the old men ride – hobbledy, hobbledy, hobbledy
> – and DOWN into the ditch.

A sensitive babysitter will quickly come to know a baby's likes and dislikes, showing her understanding by finding time to play a favorite game.

Books

You may like to share a book with your baby at bedtime. He will enjoy looking at the patterns and colors that the pictures contain, even though he is unlikely to understand the pictures before his first birthday. If you consider how very different pictures are from the things they represent then this is not so surprising – they are two-dimensional, smaller than the real thing, their textures are different and their appearance does not change depending on the angle from which you view them. Some psychologists think that being able to "read" a picture is an ability that develops gradually at about the same time as speech [48].

Having a quiet time with you as you show him a book – singing the rhymes and talking about the pictures – is something that he will come to enjoy more and more. Soon you may find him imitating you, "reading" the book aloud and turning the pages, but all the time, maybe, holding it upside down.

Board books made of heavy cardboard stand up to the sort of wear and tear that a baby of this age is likely to give them. He treats books in the same way that he treats other interesting things, banging them on the floor, chewing them and throwing them around, as he investigates them thoroughly.

Settling down

Grandparents often have the time to give their undivided attention to a baby when playing a game or reading a book, and a very special relationship may soon develop between them.

It's a good idea to keep the time leading up to bed for quiet games, stories and rhymes. You and your baby will discover your own nightly routines, with special hugs and kisses, handing over of soft toys or other treasured belongings, and your own words for saying goodnight. If you give him soft toys to have beside him on or in bed with him, he will enjoy them for what they have to offer – their soft textures and different shapes. But it will be some months yet before he realizes that they are meant to represent real babies and animals, and starts to play with them pretending they are real – feeding them, washing them and perhaps developing a special affection for a particular one.

· · · · · · · · · · ·

· CONCLUSION ·

When you look at your sturdy, inquisitive one year old and think back over the last twelve months, you may be astonished at the developments that have taken place in such a short time. Physically and intellectually she's made huge strides. She's on the point of walking and talking; she can handle things quite neatly; she understands much of what you want to convey to her and her own understanding of the world and its events is expanding by leaps and bounds.

The journey you started together is now well and truly under way and your major strength in leading her forward is that you are so often able to see things from her point of view. You know what she enjoys and what she understands and you are also able to extend her experience for her, to show her new things and give her fresh opportunities.

During the last year, many of her most rewarding explorations have taken place during the games and playful conversations you have shared together, and the coming year will open up many more new possibilities. She will become increasingly absorbed in her own spontaneous play with toys, although her richest, most advanced play will still involve you and other adults. She will play more and more frequently with toys as they were designed to be played with – snap beads will become something to fit together as well as pull apart, and not just something for waving and banging. Skills that have so far eluded her – like building a tower with blocks – will shortly come within her power. The day will eventually arrive when she holds her doll the right way up rather than swinging her by the legs – she may even put her to bed or comb her hair! In fact, sometime shortly, the whole world of fantasy, of let's-pretend, will open up for her and she will no longer be confined to the experiences of here and now.

Imaginative play

The creative, spontaneous way in which you have played with her and the amusing times you have shared together have made her aware that there is a world of imagination to explore, that life need not be limited to practicalities. The jokes and humor that are a part of her developing imagination make your games together even more enjoyable. Playing at make-believe gives her the opportunity to try out other people's roles and behavior. So giving teddy, or daddy, a pretend drink of orange juice lets her, for a change, adopt a caring role; while 'driving' a cardboard car around the floor gives her the opportunity of feeling powerful and in control. As she experiences these roles on an imaginative level, she's also rehearsing for the parts she will have to play in the real world.

Her growing understanding of language, and the fact that she will soon begin to express how she feels so much more clearly, means that there are fresh delights ahead from books and stories. She enjoys watching you play with simple hand puppets made from paper bags, making stories and songs come to life. Soon she'll start to sing along with you, making up approximations for the words whose meanings she can't possibly understand and occasionally even attempting a tune.

A variety of other forms of creative activity also become increasingly possible. She may soon be able to swim and enjoy her own competence in the water. Once she stops putting everything into her mouth you can introduce her to the fun of fingerpaints, one color at a time. You can also give her homemade playdough – made out of flour, salt and water – to use for making cakes and sausages or just for squeezing through her fingers and enjoying its squidgy feeling. Sand can be used in a multitude of ways – for pouring and sifting when dry and for molding, shaping and patting when moist. She will soon be able to scribble with chubby crayons held tightly in her fist, but her first drawing, probably a rather scrambled face, won't make its appearance until sometime in her third year.

Favorite pastimes

Outings have their own special pleasures and rituals, many of which you will introduce her to, others which she will discover for herself: walking carefully, her hand in yours, along the tops of low walls; feeding the ducks in the park; looking out for the pussy at the corner of the street; saying hello to new-made friends in the local shop or chasing after pigeons.

The wonderful thing about caring for children is that, alongside all the responsibilities and worries that it can entail, there's so much fun and laughter, as well as the sheer enjoyment of once again entering the world of baby and childhood play.

• • • • • • • • • • • •

References . . . .

1 H. R. Schaffer (Ed.), *Studies in Mother-Infant Interaction* (London: Academic Press, 1977)

2 S. Scarr and K. K. Kidd, 'Developmental Behaviour Genetics', in M. Haith and J. Campos (Eds.), *Mussen Handbook of Child Psychology* (New York: Wiley, 1983)

3 J. Kagan, *The Nature of the Child* (New York: Basic Books, 1984)

4 A. Gesell and H. Thompson, 'Learning and growth in identical twins' *Genetic Psychology Monographs* vol. 6, 1929

5 P. Zeskind and C. Raimey, 'Preventing intellectual and interactional sequelae of fetal malnutrition', *Child Development* 52, 1981

6 M. Mead, *Growing Up in New Guinea* (Penguin, 1970)

7 J. Z. Rubin *et al.*, 'The eye of the beholder; Parents' view on sex of newborns', *American Journal of Orthopsychiatry* 44, 1974

8 C. Seavey *et al.*, 'Baby X: The effects of gender labels on adult responses to infants', *Sex Roles* 1(2), 1975

9 H. R. Schaffer and P. E. Emerson, 'The developments of social atttachments in infancy', *Monographs of Social Research in Child Development* vol. 29, no. 94, 1964

10 M. E. Lamb (Ed.), *The Role of the Father in Child Development* (John Wiley, 1981)

11 J. Dunn, 'Sibling relationships in early childhood', *Child Development* 54, 1983

12 K. H. Rubin and H. S. Ross (Eds.), *Peer Relationships and Social Skills in Childhood* (New York: Springer Verlag, 1982)

13 B. Tizard, *The Care of Young Children. Implications of Recent Research* Thomas Coram Research Unit Working and Occasional Papers, University of London, Institute of Education, 1986

14 G. Carpenter, 'Mother's face and the newborn', in R. Lewis (Ed.), *Child Alive* (London: Temple Smith, 1975)

15 M. M. Haith, *Rules that Babies Look By* (New Jersey: Erlbaum, 1980)

16 W. M. Brennan *et al.*, 'Age differences in infants' attention to patterns of different complexities', *Science* 151, 1966

17 P. D. Eimas, 'Development studies of speech perception', in L. B. Cohen and P. Salapatek (Eds.), *Infant Perception* (New York: Academic Press, 1975)

18 W. London and L. Sander, 'Neonate movement is synchronised with adult speech: Interaction participation and language acquisition', *Science* 183, 1977

19 A. J. DeCasper and W. P. Fifer, 'Of human bonding: Newborns prefer their mothers' voices' *Science* 208, 1980

20 A. MacFarlane, 'Olfaction in the development of social preferences in the human neonate', *Parent-Infant Interaction* (Amsterdam: CIBA Foundation Symposium 33, new series, ASP 1975)

21 E. R. Siqueland and L. P. Lipsitt, 'Conditioned head-turning in human newborns', *Journal of Experimental Child Psychology* 3, 1966

22 H. F. Harlow and R. R. Zimmerman, 'Affectional responses in the infant monkey' *Science* 130, 422, 1959

23 Y. Brackbill, 'Cumulative effects of continuous stimulation on arousal levels in infants', *Child Development* 42, 1971

24 T. Trocianko and S. Blackmore, Dept. of Psychology, Bristol University, personal communication

25 Y. Brackbill, 'Acoustic variation and arousal level in infants', *Psychophysiology* 6, 1970

26 J. Dunn, *Sisters and Brothers* (London: Fontana, 1984)

27 T. Bower, *The Perceptual World of the Child* (London: Fontana/Open Books, 1977)

28 C. Trevarthen, 'Conversations with a two month old', *New Scientist* 62, 1974

29 E. Sidenbladh, *Water Babies* (A. & C. Black, 1982)

30 R. L. Fantz *et al.*, *Early Visual Selectivity* in L. B. Cohen and P. Salapatek (Eds.), *op. cit.*

31 M. E. Barrera and D. Maurer, 'Recognition of the mother's photographed face by the three month old infant', *Child Development* 52, 1981

32 T. Bower, 'The visual world of infants', *Scientific American* 215, 1966

33 J. L. Giwirtz, 'The cause of infant smiling in four child-rearing environments in Israel', in B. M. Foss (Ed.), *Determinants of Infant Behaviour* vol. 3 (London: Methuen, 1965)

34 S. Fraiberg, 'The development of human attachments in infants blind from birth', *Merill-Palmer Quarterly* 21, 1975

35 A. N. Meltzoff and R. W. Borton, 'Intermodal matching by humann neonates', *Nature* 282, 1979

36 Mussen *et al.*, *Child Development and Personality* (New York: Harper and Row, 1984)

37 M. E. Lamb, *op. cit.*

38 M. E. Lamb *et al.*, 'Mother- and father-infant interaction involving play and holding in traditional and non-traditional Swedish families', *Developmental Psychology* 18, 1982

39 M. Simner, 'Newborns response to the cry of another infant', in *Developmental Psychology* vol. 5, 1971

40 G. M. Colis and H. R. Schaffer, 'Synchronisation of visual attention in mother-infant pairs', *Journal of Child Psychology and Psychiatry* 16, 1975

41 J. Oates (Ed.), *Early Cognitive Development* (London: Croom Helm Ltd, 1979)

42 Mussen *et al.*, *op. cit.*, pp. 101, 102

43 *ibid*

44 E. Mueller and J. Brenner, 'The origins of social skills and interaction among playgroup toddlers', *Child Development* 47, 1976

45 B. G. Lenssen, 'Infants' reactions to peer strangers', unpublished PhD thesis, Stanford University

46 H. Weltzer, *Teaching infants infant-infant social interaction* University of Aarlius, Denmark: 1985

47 T. Trocianko and S. Blackmore, *op. cit.*

48 T. Bower, *op. cit.*, 1977

Further reading . . . .

General reference

Bee, H., *The Developing Child* (New York: Harper and Row, 1985)

Bower, T., *The Perceptual World of the Child* (Cambridge: Harvard University Press, 1977)

De Villiers, J. and de Villiers, P., *Early Language* (Cambridge: Harvard University Press, 1979)

Dunn, J., *Distress and Comfort* (Cambridge: Harvard University Press, 1977)

Dunn, J., *Sisters and Brothers* (Cambridge: Harvard University Press, 1985)

Mussen, P. H., *et al.*, *Child Development and Personality* (New York: Harper and Row, 1984)

Massage

Heinl, T., *The Baby Massage Book* (New York: Prentice-Hall, 1983)

Leboyer, F., *Loving Hands: The Traditional Indian Art of Baby Massage* (New York: Knopf, 1976)

Walker, P., *Baby Relax* (New York: Pantheon, 1987)

Movement and exercise

Levy, J., *The Baby Exercise Book* (New York: Pantheon, 1975)

Whiteford, B. and Polden, M., *The Postnatal Exercise Book: A six-month fitness program for new mothers* (New York: Pantheon, 1984). Includes exercises for mother and baby.

Play

Einon, D., *Play with a Purpose: Learning games for children six weeks to ten years* (New York: Pantheon, 1985)

Rhymes

Opie, I. and Opie, P., *The Oxford Nursery Rhyme Book* (New York: Oxford University Press, 1955)

Swimming

Whitehead, L., and Curtis, L., *How to Watersafe Infants and Toddlers* (Tucson: HP Books, 1983)

Useful addresses . . . .

Carriers and infant seats

Easily found in department stores and speciality shops.

Childcare

Your own doctor or the clinic you attend can advise you on all matters concerning your child's development.

Safety

National Safety Council
444 North Michigan Ave.
Chicago, IL 60611
(312) 527-4800

U.S. Consumer Product Safety Commission
Washington, DC 20207
(202) 634-7780

Swimming

Most YMCAs and many community pools offer swimming classes for babies and toddlers. Check your local Recreation Department for more information.

Toys

Toys similar to those found in this book can be found in any good department store or toy shop. If you have problems, the following addresses may prove helpful:

Child Guidance
Division of CBS Toys
500 Harmon Meadow Blvd.
Secaucus, NJ 07094

Fischer America, Inc.
175 Rt. 46 West
Fairfield, NJ 07006

Fisher-Price
636 Girard Ave.
East Aurora, NY 14052

Gund Inc.
44 National Rd.
Edison, NJ 08818

International Playthings, Inc.
116 Washington St.
Bloomfield, NJ 07003

Jolly Jumper, Inc.
144 Water St. S.
Cambridge, Ontario, Canada N1R 3E2

Playskool, Inc.
4501 West Augusta Blvd.
Chicago, IL 60651

Some toy suppliers who supply by mail order:

Constructive Playthings
1277 East 119th St.
Grandview, MO 64030

My Child's Destiny
P.O. Box 7349
San Francisco, CA 94120

Toys to Grow On
P.O. Box 17
Long Beach, CA 90801

Index . . . .

Acknowledgements . . . .

The publishers would like to thank
Dr. Mari Guha and Dr. Patricia Pearse
for their help and advice
in the preparation of this book;
Joanna Jellinek for proof reading;
Eileen Barry, George and Elizabeth Galfalvi
and Susan George for typing.

We would like to thank the following people
for allowing us to photograph them:
Can Akie; Geraldine Atkinson; Isabella Austin;
Martin and Stephanie Betts, and Harry;
Don and Rosemary Cowley, and Nancy;
Catherine Donnelly and Thomas; Oliver Donnelly;
Cherry Doyle and Zoë; Marian Drumm;
Emma Foale and Jamie; Harriet Griffey and Josh;
Harriet Harrison; Diane Hersee and Andrew;
Maggie Hindley and Colin Rowbotham, and John;
Andrew and Mariola Innes, Anya and Bobby;
Betty and Nigel Innes; Jo Kydd and Patrick;
Swee-Im Loh, Jenny and Kimberly;
Luxmi Manandhar, Naresh and Neena;
Michael and Susan Oruwari;
Angela and Carlo Patrono, Mateo and Livia;
Gisela and Paul Roberts, Rhiannon and Caitlin;
Kuvel and Mary Singh, and Nicholas;
Heather Thompson, Joseph and Henry;
Anna Toal and John Whiteside, and Dervla;
Sylvia Williams.

Thanks are also due to the following
for providing props and locations
for photography:
Galt Toys, 84 Fortis Green Road, London N10;
Mother and Child, 122 Golders Green Road,
London NW11;
Park Road Swimming Pool, London N8;
James Selby Ltd., 390 Holloway Road,
London N7.

Photograph on p.7 (top left) by Mike Staniford.
Photograph on pp.22 & 23 by Roger Hillier.

Illustrations by Edwina Riddell

Editor Gian Douglas Home
Art Editor Caroline Hillier
Series Editor Pippa Rubinstein
Art Director Debbie MacKinnon

Photographic prints by John Marlow and Grove
Hardy Ltd.
Retouching by Nick Oxtoby
Typeset by Bookworm Typesetting (Manchester)
Origination by Newsele s.r.l. (Milan, Italy)